the "Other" round table

EDDIE PARLOUR

the "Other" round table

MEMOIRS
Cirencester

Published by Memoirs

MEMOIRS
PUBLISHING

25 Market Place, Cirencester, Gloucestershire, GL7 2NX
info@memoirsbooks.co.uk www.memoirspublishing.com

THE "OTHER" ROUND TABLE

ISBN: 978-1-909544-53-6

DEDICATION

I dedicate this book to all those lucky people who have been involved with, or been affected by, the National Association of Round Tables. It has helped shape many people's lives, either by making the members of Round Table better and more rounded individuals or by helping to make a difference to those individuals who have been on the receiving end of any help given by the organisation. Thank you to David Brown, a fellow Tabler and inspiration, whose off the cuff remark at his 60th birthday provoked me to write this book and who has collaborated with me in the stories told, also to Chris Wardman who gave me additional stories to recount and took the time to proof read the book before publication.. I would also like to thank the following people without whom it would not have been possible to produce this book:

Bryan Patterson, Mike Peel, Peter Broughton,
Dennis Malpass, Peter Smith

TABLE OF CONTENTS

PREFACE

To most people Round Table means only one thing – King Arthur and the Knights of the Round Table. However, for many, many other people it has a separate, more important meaning and that is fellowship of what is in my opinion the greatest club ever formed for young men – The National Association of Round Tables or RTBI (Round Table Britain and Ireland) as the members know it. For these people, "The Other Round Table" is RTBI and this book is a celebration of my life in RTBI.

Unlike my previous book "Keep Up Ed!", which I was first inspired to write twelve years before I did so, this book is a relatively recent idea and came about by way of a chance remark made by my friend and ex-Round Table colleague David Brown at his 60th birthday party. My wife Linda, and I were sat with our close friend (and fellow ex-Round Tabler) Philip Avery and his wife Tricia when David joined us on one of his many "socialising" rounds of the night. He told us that only a few nights earlier he had been reminiscing with his wife Dee and had recalled an incident involving us all. Philip was (and still is) a dairy farmer and as part of a Round Table event he had thrown open his farm to all and sundry and was giving guided tours around the farm, complete with commentary. Whilst in the milking parlour he was a little put out of his stride when, completely at random and without introduction, a pantomime cow came round the corner making mooing noises! Inside the cow was David and me and after doing a quick – bad - dance we made our exit. The guided tour carried on and it seemed our little cameo was enjoyed by all – even Philip saw the funny side of it.

The point was that I had forgotten about the incident until David reminded me and I began to wonder how many other such incidents there had been that would be worth recalling - ones that involved me that I could remember or even ones that didn't involve me. This got me thinking about writing my second book with the idea of trying to bring Round Table to life, to try and get across the joy, fun and satisfaction we had in Round Table as individuals and families and perhaps inspire young men of an eligible age to join the movement. This last objective might be a little grandiose and beyond me but at the very least I would like to use the book to record my own thanks to this wonderful organisation and also perhaps to remind past Tablers of the good times they had as well.

During my research things progressed and altered the shape of the book. Thus in addition to my own personal ambitions for the book it has taken on a new objective, and that is for it also to act as an unofficial history of Mendip Round Table, the Club where I spent the majority of my Tabling life. I have recently had the privilege of viewing a history of the first 33 years (1928-1961) of Bristol Round Table No.9 with a year by year commentary written by the Chairman of that year, along with reference to previous minutes. Apart from one year, the minutes of meetings for Mendip Round Table have been lost and I have not had these resources to call upon and therefore this "history" is made up almost entirely of recollections and anecdotes and, as stated is meant to give a flavour of what Round Table is like rather than just a historical record. But by expanding my own original brief I have been able to include major events of Mendip Round Table that happened between the time of its inception in 1959 and the time when I joined in 1977, and to this end I am grateful to founder member Bryan Patterson for facilitating this information. Inevitably however the majority of the main text will by my own recollections and anecdotes that I hope will be interesting and sometimes amusing.

Like many establishments, to make the running of an organisation such as Round Table as smooth as possible each club has various offices – Chairman, vice Chairman, secretary, fund raising officer etc. Therefore it seems logical to tell the story of Round Table through tales and anecdotes roughly through the auspices of each function within the club. Where possible I have used the names of real people when relating these stories. I'm sure the reading of the book will be enhanced if the reader can personally relate to the book   On the other hand I would not like to embarrass anybody (or be sued for libel!) and therefore to avoid this, in appropriate places I have just recalled the event as best I could without naming names! Inevitably there will be some cross-over with "Keep Up Ed!", as Round Table played such a great part in my life, but I hope this tome will give a far greater insight into all aspects of this incredible organisation.

THE ORGANISATION AND HISTORY

The first Round Table was formed in Norwich in 1927. The founder, Louis Marchesi, was a young Rotarian who felt a need existed for a club where the young business men of the town could gather on a regular basis to exchange ideas, learn from the experiences of their colleagues and play a collective part in the civic life of Norwich. Eminio William Louis Marchesi was born 19th January 1898 of an Irish Mother, and a Swiss Father. He joined the Army, under age, in WW1 and served throughout the war. He was torpedoed off the Cape of Good Hope and spent 10 hours in the sea. In his letters home he called himself "Eminio", later using "Louis", but whilst in Table he called himself "Mark"

Mark became a member of Norwich Rotary Club. In March 1927 he was attending the weekly Rotary Lunch and as the appointed speaker did not turn up the then President of the Club asked young Louis to speak for about ten minutes on a subject about which he knew more than anyone else in the room: he decided to give a talk on what it is like to be a one-man business at 29 years old. He developed the idea whilst on his feet, to create a club that was exclusively for young men on the lines of Rotary but completely independent of it.

Round Table owes nothing to Arthurian Legend, deriving both its title and its maxim from a speech made to the British Industries fair in Birmingham by the then Prince of Wales who said "The young business and professional men of his country must get together *ROUND* the *TABLE*, *ADOPT* methods that have proved so sound in the past, *ADAPT* them to the changing needs of the time, and wherever possible, *IMPROVE* them." This speech quickened Mark's enthusiasm, and led to a meeting at Suckling House in Norwich on 14th March 1927 at which "Round Table" was formed. Its motto was and still is "*ADOPT, ADAPT, IMPROVE*". The founder Chairman in 1927 was Bernard Durrant.

Within a year membership of this Round Table had grown to 85 and interest had been shown in establishing Round Tables elsewhere. Whilst Round Table owes nothing to Arthurian Legend the design of the Round Table emblem is, however, an adaptation of the table which hangs in the great hall, Winchester and which is claimed to be the Round Table of the court of King

Arthur. Round Table has used the motto of Adopt, Adapt and Improve to make it an organisation which is still relevant in the 21st century. From the beginning, the Round Table was a non-religious, non-political, and non-sectarian club, an ethos that still underpins the movement today. The second Round Table club opened soon after in Portsmouth and then the idea really took off - by the time the Second World War broke out in 1939 there were 125 clubs and 4,600 members.

The first overseas group was formed in Copenhagen in 1936, and while the movement continued to grow in Denmark, the war years halted British expansion for a while. The existing clubs held strong, however, and when the war was over the momentum grew once again as clubs were chartered all over Britain. Today there are 510 local clubs, with a combined membership of close to 5,400. Sadly membership is now in decline, but at its peak there were over 1,300 Tables with about 26,000 members. However, the Round Table is now a truly international movement, with active members in most European countries, as well as Africa, the Middle East, India, Hong Kong, New Zealand, and the USA. In fact, there are Round Table clubs on every continent.

It was only very recently (July 2011) that I made my first informal visit to Norwich. I had been there in the past on a visit to the insurance company, Norwich Union on business but had not had the time to see the city. This time I was staying with friends, the husband of which I had worked with in London and who had moved to Norfolk. When we lived in Sittingbourne our friends had attended a couple of Round Table functions with me and thus Alan was aware of my interest in Round Table and was aware of the importance Norwich had had in the formation of the organisation. During our stay he suggested that I might like to make a "pilgrimage" to the site of the founding of Round Table, which he and I originally thought was the Louis Marchesi Pub, an offer that I gladly accepted. Having arrived in the area of Norwich where Alan was convinced the pub was situated, it was nowhere to be found and on making enquiries to local shopkeepers in the area we were told it had been taken over and the name changed to "Take Five". We went into "Take Five" and immediately bumped into the owner. We explained what we were looking for and it transpired that this was not where Norwich Round Table was formed, although they had met there in the past. When the new owner had taken over the Louis Marchesi the meeting room above was full of memorabilia, but this had subsequently been removed. Even more interestingly, the new owner's previous bar had been Cinema City, the country's oldest independent art house cinema, just a few yards away, and he told us that that was the site of the original meeting place. We went along to Cinema City and sure enough there was a plaque on the wall in the bar commemorating the foundation of Round Table, confirming our belief that this was the original site of Suckling House, where Round Table had first met.

As already intimated, membership was originally for young men up to the age of 40, at which time they were obliged to leave the organisation. This was to ensure that the clubs remained for young men, with new ideas being constantly generated. It needs to be remembered that when the first club was formed in 1927 life expectancy was a lot less than it is now, round about 59 years, and men over aged 40 were beginning to get old, not still in their youth as we like to think of ourselves in modern times. Over time, as numbers of new members declined and with lifestyles changing, in an effort to attract new members it was decided to increase the upper age limit to age 45. I believe that unfortunately there is no evidence to suggest that this has halted the decline in numbers.

As the movement began to grow, although membership was still within the one universal organisation with one set of rules, individual clubs were divided into geographical areas for administrative – and social - ease. There was a National Chairman with a National Council, an Area Chairman and Council for each geographical area, and within that Area would be individual Tables, each with its own Chairman and Council. A "Council" would consist of a Vice Chairman, Secretary, Treasurer and various organisational function heads such as a fund raising officer, a community service officer, a sports officer and an international officer. There would also be a Minutes secretary, to record the minutes of each meeting and anyone who didn't have a specific job would typically be stewards, to perhaps man a bar or be responsible for collecting meal money. All those who did not have specific jobs would be expected to be a member of at least one of the individual committees to assist, say, the Fund Raising Organiser to organise a fund raising event. Each Chairman, be it Nationally, Regionally or of each individual Table was in office for one year and it was traditional for the Vice Chairman to succeed as Chairman in the following year unopposed, although there were of course instances where this did not happen. Similarly, the chairman of each committee would change each year, although as will be discovered later, I did actually do two consecutive years as Treasurer in my first club to be given a chance to put right all the "cock ups" I made in the first year!

There would be two meetings each month, usually on the same day of the week, thus in my last club we would meet on the first and third Monday of each month and if there happened to be a fifth Monday in the month we would have an additional meeting. The one requirement at that time was that a member was expected to attend at least 60% of the meetings in a year, although an individual could apply for leave of absence if there was an event in their lives that they knew would prohibit them for attending regularly for a period of time, such as moving house, illness or the like. If you were away from home at any time you were perfectly entitled to attend a Round Table meeting near where you were staying, and this would count towards your 60% attendance. This was also true of any meeting you attended away from your own club, where you could ask for an attendance card to prove that you attended the meeting. To ensure vibrancy and freshness of ideas that the ethos tried to provoke, the rule was that there should be no more than two people from any one occupation in any club. However, this rule could be stretched, as it was in my own clubs, if there was a preponderance of one occupation because of the location. For example I was in a very rural area where there were a large number of farmers interested in joining, all of whom were ideal candidates (and who went on to be superb Tablers) so we had a dairy farmer, a fruit farmer and a farm manager allowed to join. We took the view that rules were meant to protect, not hinder!

Round Table would have a "business year" that ran from 1 April to 31 March and at the end of the year there would be an Annual General Meeting, usually the penultimate meeting of the year. At that meeting the Chairman and the heads of Committees would give a report of what had happened during the year and new officers would be elected for the forthcoming year. Apart from the Chairman, where the Vice Chairman would automatically be voted as Chairman unopposed, it was up to individuals to put themselves forward to be voted on as chairman of the various Committees. Anyone could put themselves forward for whatever post they fancied, except for Vice Chairman, where they would have to have a proposer and second. If there was more than one candidate for each post there would be a secret ballot amongst the active members, with those members who were due to retire under the age rule acting as tellers, as they were ineligible to vote for next year's candidates. The last meeting in the year was where the retiring members were formally recognised as leaving the club, being presented typically with tankers to commemorate their membership.

Although I believe things in modern clubs are now far less formal, in the two clubs that I attended we would invariably meet in a hotel/restaurant that had a separate room where we could conduct our meetings uninterrupted and have a meal. We would invariably wear a suit/jacket and tie. One meeting in each month would be devoted purely for Round Table business where each committee chairman would give a report and answer any questions, and the other meeting would be one where a guest speaker would be invited to give an "interesting" presentation – more of this in later chapters. It would often be the responsibility of the Minutes secretary to organise a speaker. It would also be traditional for the non-business meeting to be allocated as a day to organise visits – perhaps to a local brewery or to another Round Table Club either within or outwith your own area; again more of these visits in later chapters. Many Tablers have often voiced their opinion that of all the meetings attended they preferred the business meetings involving usually only their own members, such was the level of banter and fun that the meetings provoked.

Generally speaking, membership of Round Table is by invitation, although if an individual were to show any interest to an existing member they would be encouraged to go along to a meeting to see for themselves if it was an organisation they would like to join. There would invariably be at least one guest at meetings and from there new members were found. When the movement was in its hey-day individual clubs (Tables) would reach up to 50 or 60 in numbers and when a club reached that number of members thought was given to form a new Table in its own right from within the membership. It was considered that a Table with 50 or more members was too cumbersome and because of the limited number of posts available (Chairman, Secretary etc) the members would not have enough opportunity to get the full benefit of membership. The average age of members was about 35, with many joining at that age and thus they would have only 5 or 6 years to establish themselves and move up through the ranks to Chairman. The progress would be severely restricted if they were competing with 50 odd other members thus the optimum membership was thought to be about 30. Making the membership smaller also gave more latitude to have more members under the "any two from one occupation" rule and once the new club had reached its optimum number then in turn they would spawn another new club. Apart from new clubs being established in completely virgin geographical areas, generally it was by this method that the number of clubs increased.

When a club was formed from within an already established club, generally the members of the new club would be living in roughly the same area. The mother club of Mendip Round table was Weston-super-Mare Round Table, and Mendip was formed in November 1959 and given its Charter in 1960. In 1959 television programmes included "Rawhide", "Bonanza" and "The Twilight Zone", movies included "Some Like it Hot", "Ben Hur" and "North by Northwest". Alaska was admitted to the American union and became the 49th state and Hawaii was admitted to the Union and became the 50th State. The Boeing 707 Jet Airliner came into service and little girls loved the Barbie Dolls. Fidel Castro came to power in Cuba.

As stated, usually when a new club is formed there are a number of existing Round Table members living in a specific location within the catchment area of the established Table and these members break away and form a new Table. In the case of Mendip Round Table, it was unusual in that none of the founder members was in Round Table at the time it was established. As best as I can establish, some members of Mendip Rotary Club (situated in Cheddar) were keen that a Round Table was established in the area. A guy called Peter Hess was the "Extension Officer" of Weston Round Table and together they formed a new Round Table with new members to be drawn from the villages around Axbridge, Cheddar and Winscombe, which nestled in the foothills of the Mendip hills, hence it being called Mendip Round Table. It was the 659th Club to be chartered, thus it became known as Mendip 659.

The first meeting of the newly formed club was held at the Bath Arms in Cheddar with Keith Millman presiding as the first Chairman, Dennis Malpass the first secretary and Ken Atkins the first Treasurer. The Charter dinner was held on Thursday 10 December

1960 at the Royal Hotel, Weston-super-Mare where the toast to Mendip Round Table was proposed by Bill Porton, Chairman of Area 12 and the current Chairman, George Standen received the Charter and Chairman's jewel. In fact due to movements away from the area there were three chairmen in the first 18 months until Bryan Patterson restored some order and took over the chair for the next 18 months. Mendip Round Table held its first Ladies Night at the Webbington Hotel and Country Club. As was the custom at that time, the hotel had a "tassel dance" each night and various members went to watch the dance. After the dance two of the guys went to see the dancer to ask how she kept her tassels attached. The dancer promptly took them off, opened the guy's shirt and stuck them on his very hairy chest! I haven't been able to check if the hairs grew again. Appendix 1 lists the founder members of Mendip Round Table No.659.

The formation of a new club was a major event within an Area (that is the Round Table Area) and was a thing to be celebrated. As was evidenced with the formation of Mendip Round Table, when the Charter was presented to a new Table a formal dinner was organised with all clubs within the Area (and even those outside the Area) being invited to attend. It wasn't uncommon to have around 200 Tablers at the function, when the Charter would be presented by a member of the National Council, very often the National President but if not him then another senior member of the National Council. In the case of Mendip, although the Charter was presented by the Area Chairman, the past President of RTBI Peter Bush was present to respond to the toast to "The National Association of Round Tables Britain and Ireland".

It was traditional for the attending Tables to present a gift to the new Table, a mug, gavel or some other suitable object, along with a pennant that represented their own Table and they would receive in exchange a pennant from the new Table. Thus it was that the new Table would build up its own set of regalia. When in Sittingbourne I attended the Charter Night of a new Table being formed - Bearsted No. 1105. Our Chairman at that time was a farmer, Peter Jessop, keeping mainly sheep and our gift to Bearsted Round Table on their charter was a live lamb. It was kept in a trailer until the time came to make our presentation and when it came to out turn Peter presented the lamb to an astonished Bearsted Chairman, at which time the lamb immediately messed all down his suit! On reflection I'm not sure that was a particularly good idea, but it seemed a great hoot at the time.

To my mind one of the best pieces of regalia I have seen in my years in Round Table, and certainly in Mendip Round Table is the Chairman's chair. This was made by Doug Johnson, the first transferee into Mendip Table (who will feature greatly in this book thanks to his memories he has passed on), as a sign of his gratitude for the many happy years he had in Round Table. The Chairman was George Berry and Doug measured up George and made the chair especially to fit him, knowing that it was unlikely that anyone either larger than life or size was destined to use it. Doug caused great hilarity to George's secretary when he rang her up and asked her to measure George's bottom without him knowing so that he could create the seat! Doug duly presented the chair to the Club around April 1970 and it is still held in archive at the venue where 41 Club meets even though Mendip Round Table no longer exists.

Just as the formation of a new Round Table was celebrated so was the induction of a new member. After a suitable period of time attending meetings, a prospective member would be asked if he would like to take it a stage further and become a formal member of the host Table. If the answer was in the affirmative then his name would be circulated among the existing members and those members would be given the chance to object to his membership. Objections needed to be objective, that is to say they shouldn't object merely because they didn't get on well with the prospective member, they would need to convince the

Table executive that the candidate would not represent Round Table in a good light. Once it was apparent that the member was going to be a member he would be formally interviewed by the host Table Council and inducted at the next appropriate Table meeting. Much banter would take place beforehand, with the candidate being told all manner of untrue things of what to expect during his induction (such as he would have to bear his left breast, roll up both trouser legs, buy the beer for the next six months) but the meeting adopted a serious, reverent attitude during the actual induction ceremony. The ceremony was actually very simple, and carried out by the host Table Chairman (although if there was a National "dignitary" present it was customary to ask that person to carry out the duty). The Chairman would remind the candidate of his obligations, using wording prescribed by the Organisation, and would welcome him to the movement by pinning a Round Table badge on the candidate's lapel whilst reading out the ceremonial words. The official words were:

"You have been chosen for membership of Mendip Round Table because you are believed to be a worthy representative of your vocation, possessed of qualities which can be of service to our Movement and your fellow men.

Your acceptance of membership implies that you will carry into your public and private life the aims and objects for which the Movement stands. Your membership will involve you in an obligation to make regular attendances at our meetings and to support in every possible way the various activities of this Table.

In the name of Mendip Round Table *(John Smith)* I welcome you most sincerely into the fellowship of our Movement with the presentation of this badge. This is a symbol of your connection with a world-wide Movement of thousands of like minded men. Wear this badge at all times and remember as you wear it that you carry the good repute of Round Table into all your affairs, for the Movement is judged by those who recognize you as a member.

Fellow Members, please be upstanding. .... I commend to you *(John Smith)* and ask you to drink a toast to him. I would remind you that the obligations he has today assumed towards you and his fellow men are obligations of which you should be equally mindful".

To me it was a great feeling when I was first inducted and I made sure I wore my badge whenever I was out, changing it from jacket to jacket. Just like when you have a new car and you see innumerable versions of your car when you are driving, I was suddenly aware of how many other guys were wearing the Round Table badge and whenever I saw a guy wearing one we would invariably at least nod to each other in recognition. At non-Round Table social functions if you saw a guy wearing a badge it was customary to greet them with "Name and Table?" and instantly you had a topic of conversation to share with what was a previously unknown individual.

In general Round Table is a very informal club but there are certain formalities such as those just mentioned and the organisation does have stated Aims and Objectives. When I was in Table these would be read out at least twice a year, but always when a new member was inducted and they are worth reiterating here:

1. To Develop the acquaintance of young men through the medium of their various occupations

2. To Emphasise the fact that one's calling offers an excellent medium of service to the community

3. To Cultivate the highest ideals in business, professional and civic traditions

4. To Recognise the worthiness of all legitimate occupations and to dignify each his own by precept and example

5. To Further the establishment of peace and goodwill in international relationships

6. To Further these objects by meetings, lectures, discussions and other activities

I believe these are worthy ideals to have, but in reality as a member of Round Table these ideals just come naturally to the surface if you participate fully in Round Table activities.

To complement Round Table activities, in 1932 the wives of Tablers set up their own social networking and charitable fundraising organisation - Ladies Circle. This was originally founded by and for wives of Tablers, however it is now open to all women aged 18 to 45. Obviously I will not go into details of the Ladies' organisation here but its presence does need to be recorded, as no doubt the organisation will be mentioned – at least in passing – in later chapters. For my own part I was pleased when my wife Linda joined Ladies Circle, as apart from the fact it gave her the opportunity to have her own interests that didn't involve me it made me feel less guilty about the time I was spending on my own Table activities!

Finally, once a Tabler has reached Table retirement age (now 45), retiring Round Tablers have their own club, 41 Club (retiring Circlers have Tangent Club to join). It was called 41 Club because that was the minimum age of entry but because the retirement age of Tabling has now changed, the official name of 41 Club is now the The Association of Ex-Round Tablers' Clubs, but is still known quoloquially as 41 Club. 41 Clubs vary enormously from club to club. They have the same structure as Round Table but usually meet only once a month and are left very much to decide for themselves how active they will be. Some 41 Clubs carry on in much the same way as the members did when they were in Round Table - organising many social events, having speaker and external meetings and carrying out fund raising/community activities - whereas others like my own 41 Club merely have a meal once a month and get involved in very little else apart from the odd Area skittles match. Although some Round Tablers would have been a member of another organisation such as Rotary, Cricket Club etc. whilst still in Table, a lot of Tablers were not and then when they leave Round Table go on to join other organisations such as The Rotary Club, Lions Club, The Masons or some other such service club. Therefore they don't feel the need to have such an active life in 41 Club.

Unlike Ladies Circle, which chose to allow membership of their club to include ladies whose husbands were not in Round Table, 41 Club voted against allowing men into their club who were not in Round Table. Indeed, with the demise of many Round Tables those 41 Clubs whose Tables have collapsed have no "feeder" clubs on which to draw new members, so those 41 Clubs will eventually die out. But that is the negative side of the story. Although I am now in 41 Club I have had what could amount to a whole lifetime of experiences in my journey thus far compared to other people who haven't had the good fortune to be in Round Table ....

"HOW ABOUT SEEING FOR YOURSELF?"

In 1973 I was recently married and living in Sittingbourne in Kent and working for Scottish Equitable Life Assurance Society in the City of London (the famous "Square Mile"). !973 was the year that the UK joined the EEC, oil prices quadrupled and we worked a three day week. Lyndon Johnson, Pablo Picasso and J R Tolkien all died. I married Linda in June 1972 and we had moved to Sittingbourne, Kent, as houses were cheaper in that area and London was within commutable distance. Prior to getting married I had lived with my parents in North London and Linda with her parents in South London and thus neither of us had any connections with Sittingbourne with the result that, apart from our immediate neighbours in our new house, we knew no one where we now lived.

At work we had a guy join us from our Croydon office, called John Hajee. He and another guy already in our office, Peter Francis, were members of the National Association of Round Tables and they were always going on about things they were doing with Round Table including, in John's case, going to South Africa. John explained that Membership was open to men between the ages of 18 and 40 years (this eligibility rule has now changed to age 45) irrespective of their religious beliefs or political opinions and the only other restriction placed on the potential member is that he should either work or reside in the catchment area of which the particular Round Table is a participating organization. During our conversations the words "fellowship" and friendships" featured strongly, things that were already important to me through membership of football teams I had formed with school friends of long standing. He also explained that the old saying applies strongly to Round Table "you get out what you put in" plus you can develop yourself whilst having fun and doing good for your local society along the way. All this activity appealed to me and after a while I enquired from John as to what else Round Table was all about and he said that the best thing for me to do was to experience it myself. Without further ado he looked up the name of the secretary of Sitingbourne Round Table, who happened to be a guy called Fedor Ehrlich, telephoned Fedor and asked if he would host me for a visit to Sittingbourne Table.

Sittingbourne Round Table met on a Thursday evening at the largest Hotel in Sittingbourne, then called the Coniston Hotel. I duly turned up not knowing what to expect and was greeted by Fedor and introduced to the other members, about 30 in total. I was told by Fedor beforehand that there would be a meal followed by a guest speaker and then a little Round Table business, followed by drinks in the bar. At 27 I was certainly one of the youngest there (just younger than Louis Marchesi was when he made his maiden speech to Norwich Rotary Club, which inspired him to form Round Table) and since the maximum age for membership was 40, the oldest there would have been 40, coming up 41. I have to say that I was a little overawed by the occasion. These people were generally among the leading men in the community, many of whom had their own businesses in the area with the rest being senior members in their companies, and I was a relatively junior member of an insurance company from a very different background than these guys (or so I thought). In those days it was permitted to smoke in restaurants (although these men would not smoke until after the Loyal Toast at the end of the meal) and to intimidate me even more some of them were smoking cigars – and it wasn't even Christmas! I noticed that there was much banter and "Mickey taking" amongst the members and the evening was very funny and insightful. We listened to the guest speaker (I can't remember what the topic was), they gave away money to appeals that were put before them and talked about social functions that were being planned, we then had a few drinks in the bar and I went home thinking that it was a club I would like to join.

At that time I didn't have the self confidence that I have now and after the initial euphoria of the evening wore off doubts as to my suitability to being a member set in. Would these people accept me? Would I fit in with these people in view of our mainly different backgrounds? Could I keep up with them financially? Did I have the wit and character to join in with the meetings and get the best out of the organization? Linda told me to give it another go but I decided that I would telephone Fedor and tell him about my doubts and that I would not be going again. Fedor was horrified! He was horrified mainly because he felt these people were not like my immediate perception and that he knew that I would have no problems in fitting in (as it turned out quite rightly) and felt I would be a great asset to the organization. He persuaded me to give it another couple of meetings before making a decision, which I did, and the rest - as they say - is history. After the minimum number of meetings to qualify, which were about 4, I was formally interviewed by the Chairman (Lynn Davies), accepted as a prospective member and then in 1973 formally inducted into Sittingbourne Round Table No. 118.

Those of you who have read "Keep Up Ed!" will already know that, apart from getting married and the birth of my children, I believe joining Round Table was probably the next most significant and important thing that I did. Until then we only knew a couple of people in Sittingbourne but joining Round Table meant that we instantly had 31 other couples as acquaintances, many of whom would become close friends. Suddenly we were being invited to dances, bar-b-qs and helping to organize functions such as Bonfire Nights and other charitable events. Having joined the organisation I quickly realized that Round Table is a great leveller; when you are gathering wood for a bonfire it doesn't matter if you are the senior partner in a firm of lawyers or the owner of the local newsagents, you can still get splinters in your finger. I had always been fairly quick witted and once I realized the other guys were just normal blokes I had the confidence to mix it with them in the meetings. I was also called upon to give reports on functions, and thus I learned how to speak in front of people. Thus our social life was centred around Round Table and I found that all the members were great people and I was happy to be with any one of them, although obviously we were closer to some members than others.

John Hajee was right. In addition to the social aspects, membership of Round Table did open up new opportunities for me. Joining in and organising the various events made me a more confident, more rounded individual quite capable of talking to and dealing with anyone whatever their status, or talk in front of an audience, things that would assist me greatly throughout my life. Membership of the organisation automatically entitles you to transfer between clubs and when in 1977 I moved to the West Country with my job I joined Mendip Round Table No 659, where I stayed until I left under the age rule in 1987.

Once I had joined the organisation my life would never be the same again. To this day, 25 years after leaving the organisation, it still influences me indirectly as my social life still involves many of the guys with whom I would meet twice a month at Round Table meetings. Sadly I have let slip my friendships I made in my first Table, Sittingbourne No.118, apart from the exchanging of Christmas cards, which perhaps is inevitable when you move away from an area. However I have been living in Winscombe for 34 years now and my friends that I made when I transferred to Mendip Round Table No 659 are still very much my friends now. However, that is a long way down the story line...
....

THE
MINUTES/SPEAKER
SECRETARY

As with many meetings that take place in the working environment, when a meeting takes place involving Round Tablers then minutes of the meeting would be recorded. Sadly the minutes of Mendip Round Table have disappeared but other records show that in the early days of Mendip Round Table the Secretary read out the minutes and there was no such post as Minutes Secretary. However, in my time in the two Clubs where I was a member, this was a post that individuals would put themselves forward to undertake at the AGM; it was seen as a fun post where you could make your own impact, imposing your own style. This was particularly true with those Tables that used the position as Minutes Secretary to include the position of "Speaker Secretary" i.e. responsible for having a speaker present at suitable meetings – usually every other meeting when there was no Round Table business to be discussed.

The Minutes secretary is probably more important than is first appreciated. It's fair to say that not all members listen to everything that goes on at a meeting and those that do probably only remember a certain part of what went on. This is particularly true at a business meeting where there could be anything up to three hours of business being discussed and even the most stalwart of members will "turn off" at some time during the proceedings. The Minutes secretary cannot turn off, of course, as it is his responsibility to record all the things discussed and, more importantly what was agreed. It is particularly important therefore that everything is recorded correctly, particularly for the members who were not at the meeting. I have to confess that when I was Minutes secretary I did on an occasion or two write the minutes to reflect the way I wanted the meeting to be remembered, rather than the way it might have actually happened! Obviously, as far as I can recall, the recording of a decision that involved a vote was not recorded incorrectly, but very occasionally I felt it was necessary for a particular slant to be put on a discussion to reflect what I considered to be the best interests of the club.

It was up to the Minutes secretary to read out the minutes of the previous meeting at the beginning of the meeting. Some minute takers were more eloquent in both the content and delivery of the minutes and if they were particularly good they could get the meeting off to a good start by causing a lot of mirth and banter by delivering the minutes in their own particular style. One of our members in Mendip Round Table was Roy Norris, who joined Round Table late at the age of 37 and therefore had only three years in the Club, much to his regret. He thoroughly enjoyed those three years, particularly the banter within the meetings (to which he contributed greatly) and during one of those three years we had a particularly good Minutes secretary in a guy called Frank Brownsdon who had the knack of recording events of the evening in a humorous vein. The year that Roy left Mendip Table he produced a set of minutes for the whole of Frank's year, 1980-1981 and presented a set to each member of the Club. Reading them now it can be appreciated how they give a flavour of what happened during that year and an example of Frank's humour.

As further examples of humour that minutes have generated over the years (and also examples of Table assisting in the community, about which much more will be written later) I quote from the minutes of yesteryear:

27 November 1972 – "After discussion it was agreed to donate £10 to Cheddar Girl Guides. An amendment to donate only £7.50 was first rejected."

9 September 1974 – "After extended discussion heavy with ribaldry and innuendo George Berry was given permission to expend a sum not exceeding £15 on a 38 inch bust coat for a Wedmore lady in dire straits".

2 September 1976 – "Bob Sadler reported that as instructed in order to assist elderly persons during the strike of electricity workers he had purchased with considerable difficulty and at considerable expense ten gross of candles, only for the strike to be called off the following day. When he asked what he should do with them there was a surprising unanimity in the suggestions made".

But in some Tables the Minutes Secretary was also responsible for arranging the Speakers for the year, which is an art in itself and can result in some hilarious meetings – not always for the right reasons!

The speaker secretary always tried to arrange speakers that were informative, interesting and humorous and quite often got them all right. Being a club that was self funding we tried hard not to have to pay for speakers, promising them a meal and a respectful audience in exchange for a talk of about 30-40 minutes. The format of the evening would be that we would meet and have a meal, we would discuss any pressing Table business that couldn't wait two weeks until the next business meeting and then the speaker would be invited to speak followed by 5 minutes of questions from the audience and a vote of thanks. We thus had many speakers who would use their time to promote a cause or charity they were championing in the hope they could persuade us to give a donation to their cause, people who were trying to promote an unusual hobby and wanted to get it better known and supported, people who were enthusiastic about their hobby or pastime and just wanted to share their enthusiasm or others who were trying to promote a brand. The last category were few and far between, mainly because we wouldn't want Round Table to be seen as promoting a particular brand but we would occasionally agree to have as a speaker a local wine merchant who would give us an "informative" talk on wine – complete with samples of course.

When I was living in Sittingbourne our house was in a cul-de-sac with a Spa mini-store on the corner, immediately opposite our house. It was customary on a Saturday morning for me to get up, put on some clothes and get some fresh bread from the Spa shop for breakfast, come back, have breakfast and then shower and dress properly. One morning I went over to the Spa shop and there was an Italian chap in the shop promoting wine for a new wine shop that had just opened in the main part of town. He offered me a glass of white wine to try and was very pleased when I accepted. He asked me what I thought of it and when I said it was a little dry for me he then offered me a dry biscuit and a different glass of wine to try that was purported to be more medium than dry. This was more to my taste but I explained that I preferred red wine, which prompted him to offer me a glass of red wine to taste. Well it seemed rude to refuse so I tried that red wine and then two or three others, each glass seeming to get larger in size than the one before. After about half an hour of wine tasting I went home for breakfast, slightly inebriated with Linda obviously wondering what had happened to me (she wasn't too upset). The following Thursday I went to my usual Round Table meeting and started to regale my friends with the story when the door opened and in walked the wine merchant who I had met the previous Saturday, who was to be our speaker for the night. After the meal he gave his talk, complete with wine tasting and I felt obliged to buy some of his wares, having had so many free samples already.

Invariably the speaker would have visual aids to assist in his talk. In my day there were no lap top computers for the speaker to produce a presentation so he or she would rely on film slides, which meant needing a projector to project the slides onto a screen. This was another thing for the speaker secretary to have to remember to organise if the speaker didn't have a projector and screen of their own and sometimes the equipment was not of the highest order! I remember one such meeting in Mendip when the speaker was to give a talk on railway engines. He gave a fine introduction and we were looking forward to the slide show when, even before he could show the first slide the projector blew a bulb and there was no replacement. He then spent the entire thirty minutes remaining of his talk holding up each slide to the light trying to explain what was on each slide prefixing each one with "I do wish you could see this one…". He did get a sympathetic round of applause and one or two particularly keen Tablers looked at individual slides afterwards.

On another occasion we were being presented with a talk on Africa and it soon became clear that we would be asked to make a donation to assist in whatever particular cause the speaker was representing. The theme of the talk inevitably involved the undoubted poverty found in the African villages of the particular area of interest and one slide showed a scene of part of a village, complete with mud huts and children playing in the dirt. On top of one of the mud huts was sat a cockerel and, quick as a flash came the sound of the voice of Peter Kearnes, a very dry Brummie, with the remark "They can't be that poor, as they've got a Courage Pub!"[1] The remark was not intended to offend, as the very core of Mendip Round Table was the humour and generally speaking most speakers would

1. Courage Brewery at the time had its head quarters in Bristol, thus the beer was very popular in the Mendip area, and the brewery had as its symbol a cockerel

have had a quip back, but unfortunately this particular speaker had had a humour by-pass and he either didn't think it at all funny or he just didn't see the joke. He then proceeded to explain in great detail the level of poverty that could be found in that area and the talk proceeded to its ultimate end with no further humour either from the speaker or the audience.

The best speakers would invariably be a friend of a particular Tabler, not because they were always particularly good orators but because the members would be more sympathetic to them and we knew that we could have a bit of banter with them as if they were one of our own. One of the best speakers I can recall was a guy called Jack Lovell, the father of one of the first members of Mendip Round Table, Barney Lovell. Jack was about ninety when he came to speak to us and his subject was the Royal Flying Corps, which was effectively the name of the RAF in the First World War and was the over-land air arm of the British military. During the early part of the war, the RFC's responsibilities were centred on support of the British Army, via artillery co-operation and photographic reconnaissance. This work gradually led RFC pilots into aerial battles with German pilots and later in the war included the strafing of enemy infantry and emplacements, the bombing of German military airfields and later the strategic bombing of German industrial and transportation facilities. Jack talked for about an hour on his subject, without sitting down or stumbling over his words once and was absolutely fascinating. He explained that the machine guns that the pilots operated were set up at the front of the plane and were designed so that they would fire between the propellers, timed to fire between each rotation of the blades, and caused great amusement when he recalled that in the early days some of the pilots shot themselves down when they fired their guns and the timing was out.

On another occasion we had as our speaker a chap called David Harvey, a local vet and the vet to Philip Avery, one of the farmers in our club. This was at the time of the beginning of mobile phones being used in the UK and they were big, cumbersome things that didn't fit in a pocket. Very few of us had mobile phones of our own and we were suitably impressed when David produced one of his own and put it in front of him on the table before commencing his talk, explaining that as a country vet specialising in large animals (i.e. farm animals) this new innovation was very useful. He was well into his talk about what his day consisted of when he was interrupted by his mobile phone erupting into life and he rather sheepishly (no pun intended!) excused himself from the talk to answer the phone. He then even more sheepishly resumed his talk with a muttered apology and, again, we were impressed with the importance of this man, evidenced by the fact that he was contacted at about 10.00pm on a Monday night. David has subsequently become a good friend of mine, as well as still being a very good friend of Philip's, and he has since told me that the phone call was not for him to be given an update on a pregnant cow, which for some reason we supposed it was, but a call from his wife asking him to bring home some fish and chips! Hence the sheepish looks....

One of the strangest meetings we had was when we invited a hypnotist to be our guest speaker. His first task was to try and hypnotise everyone in the room at the same time. He was not successful in that only about 60% went under but it did give him an idea as to who amongst us was most susceptible, which was important for his next task of hypnotising individuals. He asked if anyone in the room was a smoker and wanted to give up. Martin Bull put up his hand, which was a bit of a surprise to most of us, as he was a sales training manager for Wills Tobacco. The hypnotist asked if Martin was prepared to be hypnotised and Martin said he was but would be surprised if it worked. Martin was then hypnotised and was told that when he was woken up he would be asked how he felt. Whilst replying Martin would then automatically reach in his pocket for his packet of cigarettes (in those days it was permissible to smoke in meeting rooms) take one out and light it up. He was told that the cigarette would taste so bad that Martin would put it out. The hypnotist woke Martin up by counting back from five, and then when he was awake asked him how he felt and what he remembered. Sure enough Martin reached into his pocket, pulled out his cigarette packet, put a cigarette in his mouth and lit it. He then pulled a face of displeasure and the hypnotist asked him what was wrong to which Martin replied that he must have pulled out a "bad" cigarette. The hypnotist then asked Martin to put that one out and try another, which Martin did but with the same effect. The upshot of it was that from that day Martin never smoked another cigarette, but he did in fact turn to a pipe, which he smoked thereafter until his untimely early death in 1998.

The above anecdotes are just some examples of the talks that were given at Round Table meetings. To show the wide varieties of talks that were received by Tablers there follows a list of speakers for the Table year 1980/81:

- Somerset Constabulary Driver Training School

- Veterinary Surgeon with a talk on "Animal welfare and the Factory Farm"

- County Emergency Planning Officer talking on Governmental preparations in the event of war

- An RAF Group Captain who talked on the Ultra Codes and the Enigma Code breaking system

- Nick Barrington, owner of the Oak House where we met, who was also a well known film maker, talked on the problem of blindness in the African Continent.

- A member of the Forensic Science Lab at Chepstow talked on the use of forensic science in the detection of crime.

- Two members of the CND gave a talk and showed a film on their chosen subject

- An enthusiastic collector showed some films of German war planes and the development of the jet engine

- Two members of the Cancer Aftercare Unit showed a film on the work of CARE

- A member of the Royal Commonwealth Society for the Blind

In addition to external speakers, it was also tradition for newly inducted Tablers to be asked to give a vocational talk – first hurdles as it was known – on the earliest available free Monday after induction. The reason for this is so that the new Tabler can make their first speech in Round Table and the rest of the members can get to know the individual a little better. Although it was billed as a "vocational" talk some new members chose not to talk about their work but their hobbies. In

Mendip Round Table Chris Wardman was one such individual who decided to give his talk on diving, although we were not told beforehand what his subject was. At the time I didn't really know Chris and so I was looking forward to learning a bit about him and didn't appreciate the fact that when he was introduced he wasn't actually in the room. When I first went to Mendip Round Table meetings were conducted at the Oak House, a hotel and restaurant part of which goes back to the 11th Century, located in Axbridge, a town which lies at the foot of the Mendip Hills and overlooks the Somerset levels. The Oak House had a reputation for superb food and my work colleagues were envious when I first joined Mendip Table and told them I was going there to eat and that it could well be a regular place for me to go. The room would easily hold the 30 or so members but it was of a shape that if you were at the far end you would not necessarily realise what was happening at the other end – where Chris was. After his introduction the door burst open and Chris "plopped" in, dressed from head to toe in scuba diving gear including snorkel and mask complete with flippers. His entry was similar to that of Dustin Hoffman in the film The Graduate, and indeed had the same effect as it caused great laughter. He then proceeded to give a really amusing and informative talk on his chosen sport, which I found out later was one of many interests Chris had, and still has.

By contrast, Philip Avery chose to give his talk on farming and to illustrate his talk he had different hats for different elements to the job, including a bowler hat for the AIS (artificial insemination) man. Unlike the Tommy Cooper comedy sketch, where Tommy inevitably mixed up the words and accent for the different hats on his head, Philip was very precise in his speech and to this day when a number of us get together his informative talk is still remembered.

My own "first hurdles" was a relatively drab speech. It was carried out when I was in Sittingbourne Table and I can't remember the details, but it would have been on the subject of pensions, which was my specialist knowledge at work and is in itself a dull subject. I tried to make it relevant to the members, many of whom were self employed and wouldn't have been a member of a company sponsored pension scheme, emphasising the tax benefits available. I don't think anybody actually dozed off, and I recall that at least one member asked me for more information afterwards, so it couldn't have been too bad, but not up there amongst the greats like Chris Wardman's!

As already mentioned, business meetings were often as amusing, if not more so, than speaker meetings. This was because in general the members were irreverent to each other and anyone who got on his feet to deliver a report or make a point was considered fair game to be engaged in banter. Whereas some business meetings could be three hours long this was invariably lengthened by many irrelevant comments and the speaker(s) being sidetracked. On the other hand, if the subject matter was particularly serious and members felt passionately about the subject, the debates themselves were lengthy and the quality of debate could be high, giving equal entertainment as the more frivolous debates. One business evening of great hilarity was when we decided to drink the barrel of calvados that had been given to us by our twin Table in France, Cholet, (more of international Tabling in later chapters). During one visit to Cholet we had been presented with a small barrel of calvados to mark our visit and we treated it as a "trophy" for about two years; that is it just sat in our trophy cabinet.

At one meeting it was proposed that we should sample some of this delicious nectar and a date was set when we would have an "international" evening and crack open the barrel. The evening arrived, our host had prepared a menu with a French theme to set the evening up and the first glass was poured. The calvados had been stored in an oak barrel and the liquid had taken on the colour of the barrel – it had assumed a rich red/brown hue giving it the appearance of a glass of red wine. To add even more to the likeness of wine, each member who wanted a taste was given a sample in a wine glass, with measures also being equivalent to a wine measure. However, whereas the most potent wine would be about 15% strong this calvados was an apple brandy and about 40% strong but it was very smooth and went down very easily. It is not hard to imagine the effect this had on the members and bearing in mind this was classed as a business meeting the various committee leaders still had to give their reports, with very funny results. The Treasurer gave a report on the current finances that made no sense whatever, followed by the social secretary who tried to give a resume of the number of tickets sold for a particular event compared to the number required to break even. This particular individual was never heard to cuss or swear but on this occasion the air was blue as he tried to answer inane questions from the floor, at which point the Chairman decided enough was enough and no more business would be done that evening! The rest of the evening just got more and more rowdy – in good spirits both literally and metaphorically.

We were always very lucky with our venues for meetings. In Sittingbourne I remember we were never asked to leave the bar after the meetings – indeed sometimes I wish we had been as some of the "meetings" went on very late indeed, we very rarely got home the same day we set off. In Mendip Round Table the two regular meeting places we had were both owned by current or past Tablers. At the Oak House the owner was Nick Barrington and his French wife Roley, and as already intimated the place was renowned for its gastronomy. In addition to running the hotel, Nick was also a very accomplished photographer and I believe that the hotel was at its zenith when Nick and Roley were there.

After the Oak House we went to the Penscot Hotel in Shipham, which was run by Tony Tilden, and the great traditions of Round Table were carried on there. I think it's fair to say that the food was not quite as international as at the Oak House but what it lacked in gastronomy was more than made up for in the quality and robustness of the fare that Tony put before us. Tony had a love of garlic and whenever he served up a meal that included this ingredient there were always stories at the next meeting of Tablers being consigned to the spare bedroom by their wives!

I recall that at Sittingbourne, although the meetings took place in a separate room at the Coniston Hotel, if anybody wanted a drink during the meeting they had to go to the main bar. At Mendip at both The Oak House and The Penscot there was a bar in the meeting room and it was manned by Table stewards. The job of steward was done by anyone that didn't have one of the more "senior" roles and their job was to man the private bar before and after the meeting and to collect any meal money that was due. Different Tables ran different systems to collect subs and meal money for their members, sometimes by charging for both in one lump sum at the beginning of the year, sometimes by monthly standing order and sometimes on a "pay-as-you-go" system. Invariably, however, one-off guests would not be catered for and it was the stewards' duty to collect the meal fees for those guests.

Some Tables also had one of their stewards as a "Sergeant at Arms". Whereas the formal role of a Sergeant-at-Arms in modern legislative bodies is to keep order during meetings, and, if necessary, forcibly remove any members who are overly rowdy or disruptive (the Sergeant-at-Arms of the House of Commons has general charge of certain administrative and custodial functions, as well as security within the chamber of the House), in Round Table they were invariably used to raise money for the club's charities by fining members in a light hearted way for any misdemeanours real or imaginary notified to him. In Round Table the sergeant at arms would be chosen for his wit, and he would get up at the end of the meeting and impose his fines on anybody that in his view had misdemeaned during the evening – perhaps by turning up in informal attire, had spent too long making a presentation or spoken out of turn. A good sergeant at arms certainly added to the fun of the evening but on more than one occasion a bad one would really irritate the members!

One of the traditions of a number of Tables was that of a Chairman's Night. Mendip Table adopted this after a number of us visited Weston-super-Mare Table where they were having a Chairman's evening and we enjoyed it so much we decided to inaugurate it into our calendar. The general idea was to have an evening completely devoted to something peculiar to the Chairman, be it his job, hobby or some such thing. The difference was that the Chairman would be told that the theme of the evening was one thing and he should dress up to reflect that theme whereas the actual theme was something completely different and the rest of the Tablers dressed to reflect the actual theme agreed. Since our venue host, Tony Tilden was a Tabler we had no trouble convincing Tony to put on a dinner menu to reflect the evening. For example Jeff Douce had just come back from the USA and was told that the evening was to be a cowboy evening and he dressed up accordingly. However, as Jeff was an accountant the actual evening was to be a Dickensian, "Oliver" theme with gruel being served. Steve Wilkinson, a local dentist really went to town and turned up dressed as Mr Bumble the Beadle, complete with staff and a large ledger that had been covered in talcum powder to represent dust.

In my year the theme for the evening was "Cockney" (due to me spending my formative years in London) and Tony Tilden again pulled out all the stops by providing cockles, whelks and …. Jellied eels. Whilst this was great for me, there were a number of Tablers who didn't eat any of this wonderful food. When Bill Oxenham, who was a TV producer was in the Chair in deference to Bill we made a video of a take off of the then BBC programme "Tonight", with me dressed up as Michael Fish the weather man and someone else as Fyffe Robertson. I recall we told Bill the theme was to be Hawaiian and Bill turned up in appropriate costume, complete with a hula skirt. We did actually submit this video as an entry for Gordano Vision organised by Gordano Round Table which was a spoof of the Eurovision Song Contest.

AREA
MEETINGS/FELLOWSHIP

One of the things that had attracted me to join Round Table was that I was told by being a member I would experience great "fellowship", although to be honest I don't believe that I really knew what that meant before I joined. As already said earlier in this book, when I first joined and started wearing my badge I was suddenly aware of how many other guys were also wearing the Round Table badge and whenever I saw a guy wearing one there would invariably be at least a nod to each other in recognition. This would sometimes be followed by one of us saying "Name and Table?" and a conversation striking up with what was previously a complete stranger. The thesaurus defines fellowship as being companionship, camaraderie, comradeship, or friendship and during my time in Round Table I found all of this and more, none more so than by the interaction between individual Round Tables.

There were many ways that interaction between individual Tables could take place. Quite often it would be by organised meetings within the Area but just as often it would be instigated by individual Tables taking their own initiative. My first encounter of interaction within Tables was when I was in Sittingbourne Round Table, which is in Kent, where they have a pub sport that I have only ever seen played in Kent (although no doubt one of the readers of this book living in a different County will be disagreeing with me!) and that is the sport of "bat and trap". I can't recall if the event was formally organised by the Area Executive or if it was arranged informally between one or two local clubs, but it is certainly a great way for a whole bunch of people to meet and everyone be allowed to participate in a very gentle sport.

As the game of bat and trap is so little known, I feel it is worth outlining the rules and for this I am grateful to Wikipedia. The game is played between two teams of up to eight players. At any one time, one team is batting and the other is bowling. The game involves placing a heavy solid-rubber ball, similar to a lacrosse ball, on one end of a "trap", which is a low wooden box 22 inches (560 mm) long, 5 inches wide, and 5 inches (130 mm) high, on top of which is a simple see-saw mechanism. Each player in turn on the batting side hits the opposite end of the see-saw lever (the "striker") with his or her bat, so as to propel the ball into the air, and then, using the same bat, attempts to hit the ball between two 7-foot (2.1 m) high posts situated 21 yards (19 m) away and 13 feet 6 inches (4.11 m) apart at the other end of the playing area, or "pitch". The batsman is allowed 3 attempts to shoot the ball to a sufficient height to be struck but as soon as a swing is made at the ball, the strike is deemed to have been taken. If the batsman misses the ball three times the batsman is "Knocked Out".

The bowling side stand behind and between the posts. If any of them catches the ball before it hits the ground the batsman is out. The batsman is also out if he or she fails to hit the ball between the posts at a height not exceeding 7 feet (2.1 m). After each successful hit, one fielder (the one whose turn it is to bowl next), returns the ball to the batting end by hurling, tossing, or bowling it back towards the trap, attached to the front of which is a 5-inch (130 mm) square target, or "wicket", hinged at the bottom. If the bowler hits the wicket with the ball so as to knock it flat, the batsman is "bowled out". The batsman cannot defend his "wicket" by stopping the ball in flight. If the bowler does not succeed, the batsman scores one run and continues to play. Once all the members of the first batting team are out, the batting and bowling teams change places and the game continues until all players on both sides have batted.

The rules above may not be definitive and indeed, as

intimated, there are leagues in Kent where this game is played seriously and the league itself will print their own rules, but for the purpose of this I am happy that the above rules are the basis of any game of bat and trap. When played by Round Table it was done less seriously and we stretched the rules so that the number of participants was defined by the number of people that turned up! We played in pubs that had suitable land and equipment, and it certainly engendered the feeling of fellowship. Coincidentally, "bat and trap" was featured recently to the time of writing this narrative on the programme "Country File", so no doubt it is now better known than I envisage.

Although I was in Sittingbourne Table for about three and a half years, I had very little to do with Area meetings directly and it was not until I joined Mendip Table that I became more involved. When I was transferring to Mendip, I telephoned who I thought was the local secretary, John Morse, and arranged to meet him at the Oak House where I was given a very friendly reception and warmly welcomed by the then Chairman, Ken Shelvey. I found out subsequently that John had been the immediate past Chairman and was the ideal person for me to have contacted. At the first meeting I realised that this Table was very similar to the one I had left in Sitingbourne and I encountered the same level of fellowship I had been used to. Both John's wife Nina and

Ken's wife Ann were in Ladies Circle and thus Linda also had an immediate entry into a circle of friends.

One of the additional positions within each club was Area Representative, which meant that you went along to Area meetings whenever they were held, to see what was going on within your Area, to represent your own club and put your club's vote on any issue that was raised, and to report back to your own club the events of the night. It was customary for the Chairman of the individual Table to go to the Area meetings as well but having an Area rep meant he would usually have company for the journey on the night. As already explained, each Area was set up on the same lines as each individual Table with an Area Chairman, Vice Chairman, Secretary, Fund Raiser etc thus there would be an Area meeting to discuss the business in hand in the same way as an ordinary Table meeting. For some members Area was a chore they could do without whereas others wanted the full experience of Round Table and lapped it up. Until my last two years in Round Table (more of this later) I was in between the two – I didn't want the responsibility of attending every Area meeting but I was happy to accompany our Chairman or Area rep to the odd meeting, particularly if one of them had no one to go with if the other was unable to attend.

Enjoyment in Area or at Area meetings was very much like your own Table meeting – a lot depended on the vibrancy, effervescence and character of the Chairman and his committee. If the Area Chairman was outward going with lots of fun ideas, not over-interested in rules and regulations then the meetings and events organised by Area would be fun. In my time, three Chairmen stood out for different (all good) reasons, Ian Broughal, Maurice Baker and Alan Fornier, although that's not to say I actually liked them all! Each Chairman would have his own Charity of the Year and invariably have his own ideas on how to raise money for that charity.

Alan Fornier's year was exceptional. At the time Courage brewery had a television advertising campaign for Hoffmeister beer, a subsidiary of Courage, featuring George the Bear and Alan managed to get a life sized fibre glass bear for each Table within Area. However, it was decided that it was not appropriate to promote beer and therefore the bear was known simply as "George". The challenge for each Table was to use the bear in whatever capacity each Table Chairman thought fit to raise money for his year, culminating in a central rally where the bears would all meet up and various prizes awarded e.g. most distance travelled. Alan's year coincided with Philip Avery being Mendip Chairman and we decided that we would take our George to the venue of each Table in Area, with each member being involved in the transport. This also engendered additional fellowship by the participation of everyone. At the time of the rally when all the bears congregated, Mendip Round Table caused great excitement by helicoptering George into the area of the rally, thanks to a friend of Philip who was a helicopter pilot.

One of the most common ways to promote a meeting between clubs was by way of the Table Number. Mendip was number 659 and over a period of time a "59" Club grew up, with weekends away at a central venue, often with families, where all the clubs whose number ended in 59 would meet. The regular attendees of these meetings were West Tynedale, Nottingham, Bangor, Gerrards Cross, Waltham Abbey, Newent, and Horsforth Tables. This was one of the events that, sadly for me, I never really fully got into, on the basis that in my own case it wasn't possible to do everything. I did participate in events when we were the host Table but I never experienced the hospitality that I know abounded when we were the visiting Table. Individual Tablers hosted the members of the other Tables involved and it was a relatively inexpensive way of enjoying fellowship with other Tablers and their wives from around the country. I do recall hosting a couple from Nottingham. At the time I had a rather unruly large dog, an Airedale Terrier, and many years later I met up with the Tabler when he attended a Mendip Charter Night. The first thing he said to me was "have you still got that crazy dog of yours?" so we obviously made an impression on him! As an event the popularity grew and grew and was still going very strong in 1992 when we were again the host Table. In that year the programme included a welcome and reception at the Penscot Hotel on the first day of the event, Friday 16 October, a visit to Wookey Hole Caves on Saturday morning followed by a lunch at the Webbington Hotel and then for the men only a "banner meeting" and for the ladies a swim and sauna followed by a coach trip to the American museum at Bath. On the Saturday evening there was a dinner and dance at Batch Farm and then on Sunday morning coffer and farewell back at the Penscot Hotel.

Very often, there would be a tradition within a certain Table that they would become a "visiting" Table and they would go visiting other Tables virtually every other meeting i.e. whenever they didn't have a business meeting, visiting those clubs that met on the same night as their normal meeting. It was a tradition amongst Tables to "borrow" regalia from the club they were visiting; it would only be borrowed as, as soon as they returned home they would write to the club they had visited to tell them they had part of the regalia and issued an invitation for the original hosts to go and reclaim it. This tradition was to promote visits from other clubs.

One such club was Blackwood Round Table from South Wales and we had many good evenings with them. I remember one evening when we were told they would be visiting us and we were all sat at the dining tables on our own thinking they had been held up by bad traffic, as they still had not arrived. However, we were not to know that Tony Tilden, mine host at the Penscot where we met, was in on the act and suddenly the lights went out and in trooped the members of Blackwood in single file, led by their Chairman, each with a miners' lamp on their head singing "Men of Harlech". It was a great start to the evening and when we went on a return visit to them we went in fancy dress to try and engender a similar atmosphere.

On another evening we were driving to our meeting place at the Oak House in Axbridge and we saw a number of people dressed in bright yellow duck costumes walking around town. We were mystified but assumed there was something going on involving the townsfolk that didn't involve us. It was only when we were again sat down at the dining tables that we realised it did involve us when a number of the "ducks" walked in to join us. We were being visited by Aylesbury Round Table and it was their tradition to dress up as ducks when they went visiting.

There was also a tradition in Round Table of "seeing in" a member if they transferred between clubs. This happened to me when I transferred from Sittingbourne to Mendip and a number of Sittingbourne Tablers came to Mendip to "hand me over". Later on a number of us did a return visit to Sittingbourne where we were hosted by various members and had an enjoyable evening. As has already been stated, one of the first people to be transferred in to Mendip Round Table after its foundation was Doug Johnson, in 1963. He recalls turning up at the Bath Arms where Mendip Table then met but Doug was early. Sitting on a bar stool was Ernie Toogood, well known for his forthrightness and good humour, and also his reluctance to spout unless the need arose. He once gave a vote of thanks to the Captain of Foxhounds which went something along the lines of "I should like to thank the Capt'n for talking to us about foxhuntin'. Thank ee very much". When Doug turned up for his first meeting Ernie saw Doug's badge but realised Doug was a stranger.

"Be you 'ere for Table" he queried.
"Yes" said Doug.
"I'm Ernie Toogood, Table Steward – give I ten Bob!".

Doug was hooked!

Doug transferred from Thornbury Round Table and Thornbury went to the Bath Arms for a skittles match to honour Doug when he became Chairman. Just after the game finished one of the Mendip Tablers appeared with a wheel from an Austin Mini and proceeded to bowl it down the alley on the basis that it had come off the car owned by a visiting Thornbury Tabler and it was a hilarious prank. It was only when the Tabler owner of the mini went out to his car and drove home that they realised they had taken the wheel off of a mini that was owned by a pub customer, nothing to do with Round Table, and there were frantic scenes of them hurriedly trying to put it back on before the real owner came out and discovered what had gone on!

When my good friend Colin Graves transferred to Bracknell Round Table a number of us went to hand him over and that evening was also the time of another of those great one-liners that Round Table meetings spawned. Our visit coincided with Bracknell Round Table putting on a wine tasting evening and there were about 60 of us at the meeting. To seat us all the tables had been arranged end on end in two rows, 30 in each row with 15 members sat opposite another 15 members, so the tables were fairly long. The guy conducting the wine tasting went through the usual format of getting us all to swill the wine round in our glass, then to smell the bouquet and finally to taste the wine, drawing in air between our teeth to heighten the experience. After two or three different bottles we had been through all the procedures and the guy asked us what we thought of the particular wine we were then tasting. To his mild surprise those at the top end of the table thought it tasted really good whereas those of us at the bottom end of the table thought it not so good. This obviously excited him and very enthusiastically the guy asked "so what does this tell us, why does this end of the table like the wine whereas those at the far end do not?" to which one wag came back instantly with "it goes to show this wine doesn't travel very well!"

Another memorable transferee was Peter Kearns (he of the "Courage Pub" quip), who transferred to Mendip Round Table from Llandrindod Wells, the county town of Powys in Mid-Wales. As part of his "handing over" a family weekend to Llandrindod was organised with a good number of Mendip Tablers and their families travelling up and staying in the Metropole Hotel. Unfortunately the weather was typically Welsh, with rain being the order of the day and the walking treasure hunt was not too successful. A disco had been organised for the evening, but I believe the weekend had clashed with another Llandrindod Round Table event being organised, as the number of Llandrindod Tablers at the event was rather low. However, the hotel had good baby listening facilities, which meant that those Mendip Tablers who had taken their children could relax and enjoy the evening and the weekend was a great success. That first meeting was the beginning of a good association with Llandrindod Wells Table, with members of Mendip attending an annual quiz for a number of years thereafter, with one notable night when Blackstock Round Table turned up in Dinner Jackets, bow tie and shorts!

Inevitably some Tables were more active in Area than others and particular Tables became known for the activities they put on, many of which became annual events. These events usually started off as fund raising events but over time they became events in their own right, looked forward to by Tablers from across Area well in advance of the occasion. Such events were the "Chippenham Choker" organised by Chippenham Round Table and so named because the winners of the event took home a horse collar.

Another event was the "Gordano Song Contest" organised by Gordano Round Table and inspired by the Eurovision Song Contest. This event was hugely popular and the standard of entry extremely high. Then there was the Chew valley Bed Race, where teams of up to 10 members push a bed round the 10 mile circuit of Chew Valley. In the first year we took part the prizes were to be given by the notorious Fiona Richmond, a former glamour model and actress. At the time I had just joined Mendip and as our RT didn't have a bed, as the new boy I was talked into being responsible for building one. A guy called Peter Broughton offered to help me, which was just as well, as I had no idea how to start. It turned out Peter had access to a bed and was also friendly with a local Iron worker and thus it was that he and I were welding wheels and other necessary bits to a rather large bed in the workshop of Curley Metalworks. From memory, our decision to enter the Bed Race had been taken fairly shortly before the event, as the paintwork on the bed was still wet on the day of the race. However we competed in the spirit of the race (consuming copious beer en route) and finished with blisters and chaffing in the bits where you don't want chaffing, and raised a fair sum of money in the process. Organising the event did get me known amongst my fellow Tablers however and friendships were being formed that would give Linda and me countless social events and occasions, more proof of the old fashioned social network that is Round Table.

Part of the team for the Chew Valley Bed Race

One of the most important things that Area did that promoted fellowship was the organisation of sporting events. Although I am not sportingly gifted at all, I am a great lover of sport and thus this was of particular interest to me and I participated wherever possible. As stated earlier, when I was in Sittingbourne Table I didn't get involved much in Area functions, but I was part of a fairly successful 5-a-side football team that took part in an Area competition. We set off early one Saturday morning more in hope than expectation with a team comprising, from memory, Neville Huxtable, Ron Peak, John Frewin, John House, Terry Mahoney and me. I'm sure there were a couple of others, but memory is a little vague on this. I remember that John Frewin, a very tall, slim, bespectacled optician, was going out in the evening and was only allowed to come on the basis he would be home by tea time, but such were our expectations that we expected to be home by lunch time. Things didn't quite pan out like that, however, as we progressed through round after round, including a penalty shoot-out to get to the final. Unfortunately we didn't win the final, which was even more unfortunate as John got a right ear-bashing from his wife for turning up home late!

To show how much of a sports enthusiast I am, I also took part in a team that we entered for an Area tug-o-war competition, which we took fairly seriously, having a number of strong farmers in our club. Our training was in farmer Jessop's farm yard, pulling his big Mercedes car up a gradient as our training aid. It must have paid off, however as we were rather more successful in this event and one year actually won the title.

In Mendip Table we entered all the Area sporting competitions going, football, cricket, rugby, squash, tug-o-war, but I wasn't able to participate in them all. I have only ever had one game of squash in my life, and that was decidedly calamitous, so needless to say I wasn't asked to represent Mendip in that event. I played in the various football tournaments, without reaching the heights of success achieved in Sittingbourne, and had a couple of games of cricket but was really only the last resort as I wasn't particularly good at it. The cricket was played at Sun Life sports ground (now AXA), which was a wonderful venue with excellent pitches. Some of the guys playing were really good cricketers (some even had their own bats!) and looking back my abilities were so limited that I might actually have been in danger of getting hurt by the cricket ball that I swear was coming at me at 90 miles an hour (that's what it seemed to me). But in this case it really was only about participation and we had some excellent days in the sunshine with all our families coming to watch and support. Doug Johnson recalls that in his year in 1966/7 during Mendip's innings at the Wraxall Area Cricket competition a certain Table drove a Rolls Royce across the pitch – much to the annoyance of everyone. A few months later Mendip Round Tablers attended a formal Area function at the Berkeley Hotel in Bristol where members of the offending Table were also present. The dinner started without incident but after the main course the offending Table trouped out in force to the gents to the usual chorus of ribaldry. When they returned, their table, tablecloth, cutlery and chairs had vanished completely, all neatly stowed away under the stage. Revenge is sweet!

The other sport that I was persuaded to play in the cause of Area Sport was rugby. I went to a State school in London where the only team games played were football and cricket and the only things I knew about the game of Rugby were from watching the Five Nations (Italy was not included then) competition on TV, and even then I didn't pay too much attention. But rugby is big in the West Country and most villages had a rugby team thus it was an obvious sport for Round Table to organise in that part of the country. As all the participants were Tablers and aging (in rugby terms) and to avoid the obvious injuries that could be had if the full rules were adopted the rugby played was as near to non-contact as possible, being "touch rugby". The rules adopted by Table for this game is that the normal tackles known to most rugby players were not allowed; to carry out a "tackle" the opponent had to put two hands on the player with the ball and when that happened the ball was handed over to the opposition. Whilst they explained this rule, they didn't explain all the rules of rugby, assuming the participants would know them, which wasn't much use to me. In the first minute of the first game our side attacked, we lost the ball and the opposition went down our end. Not knowing any better, I stayed up the pitch and when our side regained the ball and kicked it down-field I caught it, walked over the line and put it down for a try. Easy game! Obviously (as I now know very well) I was off-side and shortly after I was substituted, we were knocked out in the first round and that was the end of my rugby career – or so I thought.

Next year I turned up to support Mendip, but bought my boots in case someone had become unavailable or got injured, and was happy to see all our players turn up. Just before the tournament started a representative of Frome Round Table was walking round all the teams asking if there were any spare players, as they were one short. My good friend Jeff Douce volunteered my services and despite me telling them I had never played the game in my life they insisted I turn out for them. I walked into the dressing room to meet my new team mates and quickly realised that they had some good players, apparently one was a reserve for Bridgewater. I was told to go on the wing and when I received the ball to run as fast as I could. All through the first half the fly half got the ball, dummied to pass the ball to me but didn't, and I failed to touch the ball once. Things were going well, however, as we were about 12 points up, thanks to the fly half going over the line twice following his extravagant dummies. At half time he came over to me, I thought to congratulate me on my tactical running, only to be told "for f**k sake stop getting in front of me when running down the wing, as I can't pass a forward ball"! In the second half I did manage to get a couple of passes from him, but my moment of glory was snatched from me after I had dived over the line to be told by the referee that an opponent had put two hands on me as I dived over. However, Frome kept on winning and we got beaten in the final (not by Mendip, who lost in an earlier round), but I had an even bigger laugh in the tug-o-war competition that was being held in tandem. As Frome were obviously one short again I continued to represent them in this sport and they again got through to the final and won the tournament – beating Mendip in the process.

The other sports event organised by Area was an indoor sports tournament. I went a couple of times, but after the second time I never went again. The "sports" organised were on the lines of darts, skittles and other such pastimes that could be played indoors, as this was being organised on a cold evening in winter. One of the events was a pillow fight that took place between two opponents who each stood on a separate log of wood. The logs were placed about a metre apart with the participants each being given a pillow and the idea was to hit each other with the pillow and knock the other off his log, with the winner being the one to knock the other off over the best of three rounds. The current champion when I came along was the Area Chairman, a guy called Hugo King who was about 6ft 5ins tall and heavily built.

What possessed me to take him on is beyond me, as I have an appalling sense of balance at the best of times, and certainly not when standing on a log about 30 cms in diameter. As I was driving I had not had any alcohol to drink, although I was so bad I heard many of the quite large audience muttering "this guy must be pissed out of his mind". I had trouble getting on the log, let alone staying on it, and I twice quickly fell off without Hugo even swinging his pillow in anger. But mine was not an ordinary fall, where you nimbly jump off and land on your feet. On each occasion the log just went sideways from under my feet and I landed heavily on the hard floor – the arena wasn't even on a mat. I slunk away with my tail between my legs and inspected the damage I had suffered in addition to my pride. I had torn my trousers and the log had gashed my shin. Whilst that hurt a lot, I was more conscious of a dull ache in my right arm around my elbow, which got worse as the evening wore on and I had difficulty driving home. The next morning, whilst my leg was still painful I could barely move my arm so I went to hospital where it was x-rayed and it was confirmed I had broken my elbow!

This was one time when Round Table had not done me any favours, as I had my arm in a sling for a number of weeks, I was unable to drive during that time and I had to attend physiotherapy. It also coincided with me starting to wear contact lenses and I had to learn to put them in and take them out of my eyes using my left hand, which of course eventually I did. The strange thing is that to this day I still use my left hand to carry out the procedure as I find it impossible to use my natural right hand to do it.

In addition to all the other Area events, Mendip Table competed in the annual Area skittles competition, usually set up on a knock out basis, and it was after one of these competitions that I had one of my funniest evenings. It was nothing to do with the skittles evening but the fun you can get when you go out for an evening with "like minded men" that Round Table engenders. We had been competing in North Bristol and the game ended fairly early. I had travelled to the game with my good friends David Brown and Jeff Douce and we decided it was too early to go straight home. I worked in Bristol and therefore it was left to me to find somewhere to go for the rest of the evening so I suggested we went to Platform One, a relatively good class night club near Clifton Railway Station, hence the name. As we had been playing skittles we weren't particularly well dressed but none of us were wearing jeans so we looked fairly presentable. We duly turned up at the front door to be told by the doorman that we couldn't go in because we didn't have a tie on. With this Jeff got very indignant and said in his very Brummie accent "I am a chartered accountant you know. I'm very respectable" to which the doorman replied in a very condescending way "I couldn't care a less if you were the Duke of Edinburgh, you aint coming in here without a tie!"

Not to be done out of a late night drink I said that I knew of another night club but couldn't vouch for how nice it was, as I hadn't actually been in it, a smaller one off Queens Road in student-land. In an effort to anticipate any further tie problems Jeff said "leave the talking to me this time" and said he would tell a story to try and gain the sympathy of any obstructive doorman. So we went to the night club reception (no doorman) and Jeff's opening remarks were "Hello, me and my two brothers here have come down from Birmingham on work. I know we're not wearing ties but we only want a drink and no trouble, so could you see your way to letting us in?" Bearing in mind I'm about 6ft 3ins, Jeff about 6ft, David about 5ft 8ins and we looked nothing like each other this seemed a bit of a tall story to come up with, so we thought we were doomed from the start. However, the young female receptionist looked at us as if we were mad and said, "You don't need a tie to come in here, just give me £2.50 entrance fee". So we paid up, feeling slightly stupid but when we went in we could see why there was no need for a tie. The place was half empty and those that were in were obviously very young students. We stuck out like a sore thumb so we had one swift drink and went home. It's probably one of those stories that you have to be there to fully appreciate how funny it all was, but those of you who know the three of us involved will hopefully understand our mirth.

Round Table loves tradition and uses tradition as an excuse to get together and celebrate important dates. Many Tables celebrated "Founders Night", which would be either the foundation of their own Table or, more traditionally the night when it was reckoned the National Association was founded. It is also traditional to celebrate milestones of your Table – the 10th, 20th, 21st, 25th, 30th, 40th anniversary of the Table's original Charter Night. Obviously for the older Tables they would also celebrate the 50th, 60th, 70th and even the 80th anniversaries. The celebration would typically be a dinner held at a suitable local large venue with guest speakers. It is traditional to invite Tables in your Area and other Tables with whom you have had an association to join in your celebrations so it can be seen that there were many occasions when a Tabler could be out and about dining with fellow Members.

I was fortunate to be Chairman for the 25th anniversary dinner we had, which was a great success, but the most memorable one was in John Ledbury's year (1980/81), which was our 21st, but for different reasons. As already intimated it was customary to invite past chairmen to celebratory anniversary dinners along with the Area Chairman and as many other Tablers in our area that wanted to attend and so in November of that year we had a dinner attended by about 150 men. In addition to a speech from John we were to have two other speakers, including a "celebrity" to propose the toast on behalf of the guests, and past Chairman George Berry, a truly great speech maker. Martin Bull was the compeer/toastmaster for the night and we had managed to borrow my wife Linda's dad's pink jacket with tails that he used to wear as a security man at the bank of England for Martin to wear. As this was a special event it didn't fall under the auspices of a particular council member but a special team was formed to organise it, with David Brown being prominent and me also heavily involved. The evening didn't start off too well, as there weren't enough people manning the bar to serve all the people who wanted a drink, but when everyone had got themselves a drink we thought the worst was over. Unfortunately we were wrong big time. The service for food was truly appalling. We had people who got their meat but then had to wait ages for their vegetables, some who had vegetables but no meat and some who never got anything, and this continued throughout the meal. Martin was magnificent, talking the whole time, telling jokes and making light of the situation but to say the guests were unhappy was an understatement. At one time David had the manager pinned up against the wall telling him in no uncertain terms that he had better sort out the mess. By the time the speeches started it was nearly midnight and when it came for the final speaker, the "celebrity" had no chance, being on so late and all people wanted to do was go home. The whole evening was a shambles and memorable for all the wrong reasons.

The hotel in which the fiasco had taken place was part of a well known chain and we wrote to the Managing Director explaining what had happened and asking him what he intended to do, before we paid the bill. They agreed to send their Area Manager to a meeting with a select representative of Mendip Round Table and in due course a meeting took place at the offices of Hill Samuel (a Merchant Bank, now part of the Lloyds Group), where John Ledbury was a manager and where I was also present. The Area Manager introduced himself as "John Spangle, as in the sweet" to which I replied "Hi, I'm Eddie Parlour, as in beauty". That rather set the tone for the whole meeting, friendly but with us making it clear that we wanted some sort of recompense. In the end it was agreed that all we would have to pay for the evening was the hire of the room and the staff wages, with effectively them letting us off about £1,000! We thought this was a very fair compromise and wrote to every guest offering them a refund or asking if they would like to donate their share to charity. Only a handful of guests opted for a refund and that year turned out to be one the best fund raising years we had ever had.

As I say, four years later I was Chairman for the 25th anniversary, which took place on Monday 14 October 1985. Although the chain of hotels we had used for the 21st Charter had redeemed themselves by the way they had handled our complaints at that time, we decided to go to a different venue for our 25th, which took place at the Mendip Hotel at a cost of £11.85 to guests, £7.85 to then current Mendip Tablers. I am pleased to say that the evening went off without any major hitches. However, in true Round Table fashion everything took a lot longer than had been planned for and once again the speeches started late. Thankfully for everyone concerned I cut down my speech to about 5 minutes, but it was still a late evening. I was lucky to have a number of past chairmen and founder members at the dinner, although unfortunately not as many founder members as I would have liked. The organising committee had the foresight to engage a photographer for the occasion and I also had the foresight to order copies of the relevant pictures, some of which are reproduced here.

*Mendip Round Tablers 1985-86 at 25ᵗʰ anniversary dinner.
The 2 guys in light coloured suits were Cholet Tablers who visited
us for the celebrations*

*Me as Chairman with founder members of Mendip Table at 25ᵗʰ
anniversary dinner. Back row l to r Keith Smith, Richard Patterson,
me, John Horne, Ivor Standen. Front row l to r Geoff Rodway,
Bryan Patterson, Dennis Malpass*

Me as Chairman with those past chairmen of Mendip Table present at 25th anniversary dinner Back row l to r Richard Brown Derek Evans, Steve Tilley. Centre row l to r Ian Leavey, Ken Shelvey, Peter Smith, John Rose, John Morse, Mike Phillips, Bill Oxenham, John Horne, John Ledbury, Jeff Douce. Front row l to r George Berry, Barney Lovell, Doug Johnson, me, Bryan Patterson, Dennis Malpass

In my last year in Round Table I fully engulfed Area when I stood for the position of, and was elected, Area Extension Officer, or to give it its alternative title, Area Membership Officer. I was approaching the magic age of 40 and thus in my last year in Table, had just completed my year as Chairman and didn't want to feel like a spare part in my last year, just waiting for the time to come when I left this great organisation. During my time as Chairman, as one of my duties I attended Area meetings and therefore as I had had a year of Area involvement it was quite an easy transition to join the Area Executive.

The role of Area Membership officer, as I saw it, was to encourage Tables within Area to increase their membership, to help them in any way that I could with any promotional ideas that they had to fulfil this objective, and to help save any Tables that were suffering from lack of membership and were in danger of folding up. During my time in Mendip Table I had introduced a number of people to Round Table, so it seemed a natural role and a fitting end to my career in Table, to try and preserve something that meant a great deal to me. In Mendip I had never had any trouble introducing people to Round Table. Shortly after moving into my home in Winscombe Linda was invited to a social evening with local young mums, to include their husbands, and I was introduced to Ken Brown, who was to become a really good friend and my first convert to Round Table. It seemed natural for me to want to share with guys that I liked the opportunity to join a great organisation such as Round Table and I guess my enthusiasm must have rubbed off, as very shortly afterwards I was introducing Mike Peel. Both Ken and Mike proved to be really super Round Tablers, still coming to 41 Club, but I'm pleased to say that there were many others I influenced, either directly or indirectly to join Mendip during my time with them.

During my year as Area Membership officer I visited all the Tables in Area 12, some twice and was warmly greeted wherever I went. At the same time that I was Area Extension Officer my very good friend Peter Smith was also on the Area Executive, being in charge of Area Shop, a role at which he was very successful. There were many times we travelled together to the various locations, thus it really was no hardship travelling all over our sprawling Area. In my year there was one Table that was struggling to survive and in my eyes my greatest success during my time as Area Extension Officer is that at the end of my year the Table was still in existence and remained so for a few more years.

COMMUNITY SERVICE
AND FUND RAISING

In Round Table these two offices are separate with different Chairman but I have included them together in one chapter, as very often they are inextricably entwined and one function can impact on another. For example it could be argued that the Axbridge Air Disaster (much more about this later) started off as a fund raising exercise but it became far more than that as Round Table ended up carrying out true community service work.

Long before I had the pleasure of joining Mendip Round Table the members were involved in community service and fund raising. Just four years after Mendip Round Table was formed, on 26 July 1963 a huge earthquake measuring 6.9 on the Richter scale struck the city of Skopje, which was the capital of Macedonia on the banks of the Vardar River, then in the republic of Yugoslavia. Over 1,000 people were reported killed and

200,000 made homeless. Following an announcement on TV by Richard Dimbleby on the plight of the homeless, Mendip Round Table raised money to buy a caravan, which obviously needed to be transported to the stricken area. Names were drawn from a hat and the four names drawn were Bryan and Richard Patterson, Richard Brown and Barney Lovell. In addition to the caravan, Macedonian students from Bristol University gave supplies to pass on to relatives. The four Tablers set off in November 1963 in a Wolseley 6/90 (people might remember it as one of the cars used by the police) but the car and van were so loaded with provisions, including a stove, that it boiled over going up Cheddar Gorge and had to be pushed! Our four intrepid adventurers also had to push it up the Alps later on in their journey.

The whole trip lasted one week, with all four driving in rotation non-stop on the way there apart from midnight to 5.00am, with sleep being taken in the car. It took three days to get to the appointed drop-off zone and on the way back they stopped for one night in a hotel in Belgrade, where they went to the Crystal Ball Night Club. From there they went to Trieste then on to Innsbruck where they were all persuaded to buy night dresses for their wives as a going home present. The final part of their journey was from Innsbruck to Calais and home to their families.

Three years later at 9.15 am on Friday, October 21, 1966 after several days of heavy rain a waste tip slid down a mountainside into the mining village of Aberfan, near Merthyr Tydfil in South Wales. It first destroyed a farm cottage in its path, killing all the occupants. It was sunny on the mountain but foggy in the village, with visibility about 50 yards. Down in the village, nobody saw anything, but everybody heard the noise. At Pantglas Junior School, just below, the children had just returned to their classes after assembly. The slide engulfed the school and about 20 houses in the village before coming to rest. Then there was total silence.   144 people died in the Aberfan disaster: 116 of them were school children. About half of the children at Pantglas Junior School, and five of their teachers, were killed. Nobody in the UK living at the time will ever forget the scenes of devastation and although this time Mendip Round Table was not able to offer on-the-spot assistance, help was given by donating to the relief funds that were organised. Various members of the club made collections by going from pub to pub in the Mendip area collecting money and sending it on. One contingent, including Doug Johnson went to the Webbington Country Club during a live show and filled several buckets with cash.

Just close to Winscombe, one of the many villages home to the members of Mendip Round Table is Barton

Camp, a residential centre nestled within the beautiful rolling hills of the Somerset countryside and is also the home of the Bristol Children's Help Society, which has been operating in one guise or another for more than 120 years. Run entirely by volunteers, the centre offers free or heavily subsidised holidays within a safe and happy environment to thousands of disadvantaged children from across the south west every year, giving them much-needed respite from their often very difficult lives. For many of these children, it's the first holiday they've ever had. One of the earlier members of Mendip Table, Tony Fowles, had been to this camp as a child and as he progressed in life and became a very successful business man he never forgot the good times he had at Barton Camp and did all he could to support their cause. One of the things he did was to do a sponsored walk along the M5 - before it opened – from Weston-super-Mare to Clevedon with the proceeds going to the camp. Over the years both during his time in Round Table and even after he left, Tony has influenced the fund raising of Mendip Round Table to continue to help this cause.

The fund raising events of Mendip Round Table have been very varied over the years. Again, long before I joined the members proved to be an ingenious lot, using the local facilities and dreaming up different ways to raise money for local and national causes. One of the first events was the Miss Mendip dances held in Birds' Assembly Rooms in Winscombe. As the title suggests, this was a dance that also included a beauty parade, open to any female in the area to find "Miss Mendip". Older members recall that they had to have people on the door to stop the local ruffians from coming in and disrupting the proceedings.

Another innovative scheme dreamed up by my forebears was a Christmas float. This was a model of a church that was illuminated and then paraded round the local villages, with carols relayed by a sound system and passers-by/ local inhabitants invited to make donations for Mendip Round Table local charities. This float was built in one of the members' garage but unfortunately they didn't check the dimensions before or during the build. The result was that the float, when finished, was too big to get out of the garage. Rather than dismantle the float, they decided to take the doors off the garage and were able to get it out that way. Unfortunately records do not exist to show the total amount of money raised by these events overall, but it is known that in 1965 during Richard Brown's year £60 was raised by this function.

Also in Richard's year a "Rotable" (a joint event between Rotary and Round Table) fete was held at the Kings of Wessex School where £250 was raised, a Gymkhana at Palace Farm in Wells raised the grand sum of 16shillings and 6 pence (82.5 new pence), a jumble sale, also at Birds Assembly Rooms raised £49.20 and a "Pile of Pennies" in the Bath Arms raised £13.30 in aid of Cheshire Homes. The Rotable event took place on other occasions and Doug Johnson recalls that in his year in 1966 it rained so hard in the morning that Cheddar was flooded. However the weather turned for the better by 2.00pm and all went well with dozens of stalls to suit all tastes, including seven teams competing in a piano smashing contest against the clock. Prior to the event Doug and Richard Brown waited until very late in the night to meet a guy called David Lafferty who had just spent 143 days solo underground in Cheddar Caves to achieve a world record, to secure his agreement to return to Cheddar a month later to open the fete along with Miss TWW (Television Wales and West) Sally Alford.

The jumble sale was also an event that took place on other occasions. Doug recalls that in his year in the Chair, Peter Duckett was on the shoe stall and sold a female a pair of shoes. She duly sat down to try them on only to find a condom in one of the shoes! Despite Peter's protestations he was unable to convince her that he was not the culprit.

In the late 1960's, as has already been mentioned, the M5 had not been built and traffic on the A38 going to and from the West Country through Cross,

Winscombe and Churchill Crossroads particularly on Bank Holidays was immense, with traffic jams the like of which are seen now only on the occasion of a bad accident. Not ones to miss a trick, Mendip Tablers decided to raise money for charity by building a hot dog stall and selling their wares from Cullen's Garage (now Budgens) on the A38 to passing motorists who were stuck in the traffic jam. Initially the food was prepared from a horse box using gas bottles and gas burners, but as time went on they converted other transport to make them look more professional. During Richard Brown's year £84 was raised, not a bad sum of money in that era.

In 1969 during Jim Lukins' year as Chairman one of the most prestigious fund raising events was inaugurated – the Traction Engine Rally. Not being a member in those days, when this story was relayed to me I was surprised to learn that Mendip Round Table had to supply the coal for all the engines, which Bryan Patterson managed to secure with no cost to Table. From this first event Jim recalls that they raised £1200 that year. Obviously the event was a huge success, as at the second Rally and Show held in conjunction with the Somerset Traction Engine Club at Cheddar the event was run over three days on the Autumn Bank Holiday and attracted a crowd of 12,000. A profit of £2,282 was made, the majority of which was given to four local charities – St Michael's Cheshire Home ((£700 to a new Chair-Lift Bus), Weston-super-Mare Spastics (£500 towards a swimming pool), Badgworth Court (£500 towards a new kitchen) and Cheddar St John's Ambulance (£350 towards a new ambulance). These were huge sums of money in those days, particularly for a relatively small club to raise and members were rightly proud of their achievements.

Then came the event that, for me, defines how Round table is able to help communities, albeit brought about by something that everyone hopes will never happen again. On Tuesday 10 April 1973 at about 8.30am a plane took off from Lulsgate Airport carrying 145 passengers and crew bound for the Swiss city of Basle. At 10.10am Basle air traffic control lost touch with the pilot of the Bristol flight on its landing approach. The plane had ploughed into a snowy, forested hillside near Basle, somersaulted and broken up. Some in the rear section of the aircraft survived the crash almost unscathed and two, Bristol headmaster Barry Rogerson and a teenage boy set out to raise the alarm. By midday news of the disaster had reached Bristol and by early afternoon it was confirmed that more than 100 had died in the worst loss of life the Bristol area had suffered since the Good Friday blitz 32 years earlier. In one heart-breaking moment fathers had lost their entire families, scores of children their mothers. The presence of so many groups of women friends and neighbours bore down heavily on small towns near Bristol like Axbridge, Cheddar and Congresbury where the day trip to Basle had been such an exciting date on the calendar. The final death toll was 108.

The crash coincided with the start of a new year in Mendip Round Table and consequently a new Chairman in Richard Harrill, who had taken over from John Horne only the previous day, and a new committee. A young Ian Leavey had just been elected Community Services Officer but it was felt unfair for such a new member to have to shoulder the burden of what was obviously going to be a huge task in helping with the disaster, so the position became a "Table" position. Mendip Round Table gave enormous help to the rescue authorities and at the 1973 National Conference asked the National Association Of Round Tables for funds to start an appeal fund for the victims of the disaster, prior to which Richard had sent an Appeal Letter to each Table Chairman. Indeed everyone in Mendip Round Table knew someone who had lost a relative in the air crash so it was an emotional time for all the members. I feel I can do no better than to reproduce the speech given by Richard at National Conference, as this sums up exactly what happened and, even now, conveys the raw emotion felt by all in our Table.

"Tuesday 10th April 1973 is a date that will be

implanted forever in the minds of members of Mendip 659, for as you know on that day our area suffered a tragic disaster. A plane carrying 139 passengers plus 6 crew left Bristol Lulsgate Airport for a day trip to Switzerland, and crashed into the hills of Hockwald. Of the passenger and crew 108 people died. The remaining 37 survivors suffered injuries of varying degrees from the extremely serious to the few fortunate who were practically physically unscathed.

The impact on the community at the first somewhat sketchy information available was devastating. Mendip Round Table's involvement started immediately at a hotel in Axbridge owned by a Tabler, where some of us gathered together to see if we could be of any assistance to anyone who needed aid. It was soon obvious that there was no central official place to which these distressed relatives could go to obtain information or assistance and an organization between Round Table, Lions and Rotary just seemed to spring into existence that afternoon.

A liaison was set up between us and Invicta Airlines at London – Special Branch at Lulsgate Airport – Telex to Switzerland via a local Testing Station – the Government via our local MP at Westminster – the local police – Clergymen and local Parish Councils, and before long we seemed to be the complete centre through which everything passed.

As this was a charter day trip the date of which had

been altered only a fortnight before, a list of those who had actually made the trip was not an easy thing to collate – a lot of tickets had been booked in the organizer's name, there had been people cancel from the first date and their places taken by others, and some people had not booked through the local travel agent at all. No complete list of those on the organized trip had been left and the organizer had perished in the accident. Obviously the first concern was to get a flight plan but this was not forthcoming for two whole days, by which time we had already made our own investigations and collated the necessary information.

Lists of survivors began to come in slowly, but great care had to be taken before releasing any information as there were similarities of name amongst those on the plane, and wrong information could only cause unnecessary suffering – so great care and discretion had to be used. Unless positive information was available we could only inform relatives that there was no information available at that present time.

Relatives were waiting at our centre or constantly ringing in all through the first night and forthcoming days and nights. A flight was arranged to take to Switzerland anyone who wished to go to enable them to identify either living or dead passengers. This could either be booked through us or Invicta Airlines in London. We booked 106 of the 150 people who went out on the two flights on Wednesday 11th. We had two and a half hours notice of take-off and had to contact, collect, and get these people to the airport. Arrangements had been made by us for passports and vaccinations, but these were eventually waived by the Immigration authorities. £500 had been drawn and changed into Swiss Francs to cover immediate expenses by those on board these two flights. Arrangements were made to look after any children that were being left behind, and local clergymen traveled out with the relatives.

Basle Round Table, Rotary, Lions and Salvation Army had been contacted and had assured us that everything the other end would be taken care of. Meanwhile a Joint Community Committee was set up to provide meals and entertainment for the children. Ladies Circle, wives of Tablers and WRVS ensured that the children and families were fed and cared for. By the Thursday the vast number of calls into the centre had been recorded and listed into categories of the types of help and assistance offered. Record cards had been made for all persons on the disaster flight, noting next of kin, doctors, dentists, solicitors, children and all other personnel details which we had been able to gather.

On the Thursday morning we in fact had seven phones permanently in use. We had had to set up a further office across the road in the cottage which we were lent, and intercom between the three offices was installed. On the Thursday evening we received a flight back from Basle with 178 passengers on board a DC10, which was too large to land at Lulsgate, and was brought into RAF Lyneham. We took five coaches to Lyneham and when we arrived there set up yet another office provided by the RAF with a phone link to Axbridge in order that immediately the plane landed we could let them know exactly who had returned, as there were anxious relatives awaiting this news. RAF Lyneham arranged security to protect passengers from any outside disturbance. Half an hour before the plane landed we were told that we were to expect four stretcher cases and several other walking survivors. We had previously taken the precaution of providing ourselves with five trained nurses to cover any eventualities which might arise on the return coach journey with distressed relatives. We were able to spare three of these for ambulances which we borrowed from the RAF and the other two came back with the couriers on the five coaches. At the end of the journey which was 2am Friday morning we were met by Tablers and Rotarians with cars. Arrangements had been made for local doctors to be on standby and in one instance it was found necessary to call upon a doctor to give sedation.

Several more flights of a similar nature had to be arranged during the ensuing days, especially in regard to those survivors on the critical list. By the Friday we had two members of Kenyons International Funeral Directors with us. They are specialists in disasters and came to Axbridge to work with us, and the unpleasant task of obtaining identification particulars had to commence. Bereaved families had each to be visited to obtain all personal information which could be of any assistance to the team of pathologists working at Basle, together with details of nationality from the Grandparents down. This was indeed a most distressing task and other Tables were contacted for assistance in several cases where next of kin lived outside our Area. Further arrangements for bringing back the coffins were also put in hand during that weekend.

Three representatives went from the Axbridge Disaster Centre out to Basle to liaise with the Presidents of Round Table, Rotary and Lions, and arrange a direct Telex link with us in order that we might receive daily hospital reports on all survivors during their entire stay. Clothing and personal effects were obtained for those in hospital and British Consul arranged for newspapers and daily visits to be made to the hospital, carried out by the British Circle in Basle.

During the first frantic weeks we did not close the centre day or night, and those of us who had been on duty from the start had experienced something very soul shattering. Of course, the hectic pace has abated now that the funerals and memorials are over. Social Services have now taken over some of our work, and we are operating an office with the aid of two secretaries, in accommodation provided by them, but now the real lengthy task begins, trying to aid fathers left with children, trying to help with the children themselves, and this brings me to my Appeal Letter.

As I stated in this letter to all Table Chairmen, I did not immediately launch a National Appeal. The reasons for this were twofold, I felt it necessary to make investigations concerning legal matters, and I also wished to avoid an accumulation of funds which might become an embarrassment if they were not needed. On investigation the necessity for an appeal became apparent. I would like to put you in the picture as to the present position:-

At present there are five survivors still in Basle Hospital who are likely to be there for many weeks to come and two visitors per patient are being flown out every weekend. Volunteers take the visitors to London Airport where they are taken over by Invicta Airlines who fly them out to Basle. A certain amount of cash has already been distributed to alleviate immediate financial hardship, and daily the secretaries are receiving requests and passing on information to a committee formed by Table, Rotary and Lions and called the RRL Committee, which consists of the original members who started the Disaster Centre.

The purpose of this Committee is to ensure that each family affected by the disaster is visited first of all weekly, then fortnightly, and subsequently perhaps monthly, to maintain contact in order that on each visit any problem which might have arisen can be discussed and help offered where needed. This help of course can be financial or with such things such as Solicitors, Insurance and the many varied things which will crop up over the coming months. It is the aim of this Committee to help in any way possible and to put to use the many offers of assistance we have received.

These offers of help have been many and varied, from offers of holidays for fathers and children, babysitting, help with washing or cooking, transport etc.etc. Of course this disaster will have long term effects – after all there were 87 children involved who either lost a parent or parents, or had a parent on board which was a survivor. Even those survivors who were not severely injured have sustained a severe emotional shock.

I have endeavoured to give you, gentlemen, a report of what has happened since that ill fated day of 10th April; this is an impossible task, there is so much that has happened that just cannot be put into words.

In concluding I would like to thank the Tables of Bristol, Westbury on Trym, Bath, Gordano Valley, Weston-super-Mare and Thornbury for their assistance in providing transport and obtaining identification particulars, and to all Tables for their offers of help and assistance. Much help will still be needed in the future, and I shall not hesitate to ask when the need arises. The night before this disaster struck I was installed as Chairman of Mendip, and in my speech I said that my theme for the year was fellowship – as this word embodied community, social, fund raising – in fact fellowship covered it all. Little did I realise what a tremendous lesson in fellowship we were to experience over the ensuing weeks. It has been gratifying to all of us in Mendip to experience the fellowship of RTBI and to know that there is such a fund of help both practical and financial so readily available.

Gentlemen I thank you all."

I feel that what my Round Table predecessors did in the wake of the air disaster was absolutely astounding. In these days of home computers and instant communications the work they did would have been impressive enough, but remember these relatively modern inventions were not available then and there were no such things as mobile phones. Indeed although Subscriber Trunk Dialling (STD, the process to allow a caller to call another telephone directly instead of via a manual telephone exchange operator) was first introduced in 1958 it wasn't until 1979 that the process was completed. These days if there were again such a disaster there would be governmental organizations in place that would, or should, undertake a lot of the work that Mendip Round Table and their colleagues did at that time, although I am sure there would still be a lot that the local Service Clubs would be able to do.

The work of the Committee carried on and, in November 1973 a delegation from Axbridge visited Basle, the delegation comprising Richard Harill, The Venerable J. du B. Lance (Archdeacon of Wells representing the Bishop of Bath and Wells), Mr. J G Walter (Chairman of Hochwald Disaster Funds and Chairman of Axbridge Rural District Council), John Lane (President of Mendip Rotary Club) and Mr. R Evans (President of Cheddar Vale Lions Club) plus three representatives of Invicta International Airlines. The delegation flew out on 6 November and over the next three days they attended various presentations along with various local dignitaries at the Consul, the Church at Hochwald and hospitals where speeches were made, plaques were unveiled and oak benches presented. Two oak saplings were planted, including one at the actual scene of the accident where a memorial was to be subsequently erected. The delegation returned on Thursday 8 November.

As stated earlier, I joined Sittingbourne Round Table in 1973 and after a short while I also started to realise that through Round Table I could help make a difference to others less well off than myself and indeed start to give back something to the organisation that had helped me so much, and two things stand out during my time in Sittingbourne, one nationally and one locally.

The national help that I was involved in was the Anthony Nolan Appeal, and I quote from their website from the time that I wrote "Keep Up Ed", which I believe best explains the situation: "In 1971 Anthony Nolan was born and found to be suffering from the very rare Wiskott Aldrich Syndrome (WAS), a rare inherited immunological disorder affecting around four male babies in a million. In 1973 the world's first bone marrow transplant was performed using an unrelated donor - previously, transplants had always been taken from a relative of the patient. The success of this operation quickly became the foundation for Anthony's mother Shirley's vision. In 1974 Shirley established The Anthony Nolan Register in the basement of Westminster Children's Hospital, the organisation's first home, under the direction of Dr David James. Dr. James was a consultant pathologist, responsible for the donor testing programme at Westminster Children's Hospital where Anthony was a patient."

It was Thanet Round Tablers that helped in the establishment of the Register for tissue-typing and this marked a long and illustrious history of support from

The Round Tables of Great Britain and Ireland. As explained previously Round Table was divided into Areas and Thanet Round Table was in the same Area as Sittingbourne. Tissue-typing was then, as it is today, a complex and expensive process and I am proud that I was with Sittingbourne Round Table that helped raise funds to assist in establishing this trust.

On a local front we organised the local Fireworks display on Guy Faulkes Night that raised thousands of pounds, took part in the annual Town pageant and also organised the largest New Year's Eve ball in the area. Guy Faulkes night was my first big fund raising venture in Table and was extra important, as it was an ideal opportunity for me to get to know my fellow Tablers away from the fort-nightly meetings. It needs to be remembered that this was 1973 and there wasn't the same concerns about "health and safety" with the result that we had a bonfire and everything was controlled by Round Table, including the setting off of the fireworks. I can't recall exactly where we obtained our firewood from but eventually it was put in the middle of a field on the Saturday night before 5 November. We finished stacking it about 5.00pm and I volunteered to stay with it to ensure nobody came along and set it on fire before the proper time – another task given to the "new boy"! I was almost pleased to see a guy walk towards me, as it was getting a bit lonely, but I thought I had better still challenge him in case he was up to no good. He wasn't amused however, as it turned out it was his field we were in! Whilst we were talking my fellow Tablers began to turn up to set up the firework area and I went home to get some dinner before returning to take up my responsibilities on car park duty. Getting the cars in wasn't too difficult but getting them out wasn't so easy. We had already had a fair bit of rain during the week and more rain fell during the evening, so there were quite a number of cars that got stuck in the ensuing mud. Fortunately we had a few farmers in our club and, anticipating the potential problems, we had a couple of tractors on hand to pull them out. I haven't got records of the exact amount of money raised but it was regularly our biggest fund raising event of the year.

The annual Sittingbourne Town pageant was a summer event and consisted of local people preparing and parading floats. We in Table decided to enter our own floats based on Disney characters. Quite understandably the Disney Corporation would not give us permission to call our effigies after Disney characters, as they had no control over how good we would recreate them, so we built them and entered them merely as animal characters. I had never been involved in making anything like this, but soon I was totally engrossed, spending most of my spare time in various barns where the characters were being built. All of the characters were built out of papier-mâché on a chicken wire frame and the ones that were to be carried individually had a rucksack frame as a base. Once the papier-mâché had set the animal was painted and then had a coating of clear varnish applied to ensure it was water-proof. Our biggest model was a pink elephant with a hat on, with a mouse on that, which was on wheels. It was large enough to have two men inside it pushing and was a real work of art. The animal that I worked on the most, and really became my "baby" was a goofy like character, complete with a tall hat. I am about 1.90 mtrs (6 ft 3 ins) tall and with the head on I stood about 2.4 mtrs (8 ft). Parading it around Sittingbourne in the pageant I regret to say that I did frighten a few children and made more than one dog bark

For some reason I had always enjoyed New Year's Eve celebrations the most of all the Christmas festivities so when I found out that Sittingbourne Round Table organised a New Year's Eve party I was more than happy to be involved in the organisation. It took place in the Town Hall and consisted of a dinner dance with catering carried out by the local Army Catering Corps and music by the Jack Whitnall Band, a local group that was regularly used by Table and well known locally for its quality. About 150 people were catered for with formal dress (DJ etc.) being the normal attire. At midnight it was traditional for Sitingbourne Tablers to put on a short cabaret so I was regularly missing as the clock struck 12. It was at one of these dances that I first met Peter Smith, who was in Whitstable Table and who transferred to Mendip Table shortly after me, although at that time I wasn't to know how good a friend he was to become. Peter, me and a few other Tablers decided to dance around the floor amongst the other dancers in a line in the style of Pan's People (the well known female dance troupe that regularly appeared on "Top of The Pops") – it seemed a good idea at the time! The New Year's Eve Ball was a huge success looked forward to by many people in the area and we never had trouble selling tickets.

Also in Sittingbourne was a local operatic society that would regularly put on concerts in the Town Hall. For most of these concerts the society would charge people to attend but for one night they would put on a concert for the elderly completely free. As one of the largest organisations in the area, Round Table would be drafted in by the local Age Concern/Help The Aged organisations to collect the elderly residents of Sittingbourne and surrounding areas from their homes (mainly female), take them to the Town Hall and then after the performance take them back home.

As one of the volunteers I was given the addresses of three elderly ladies to collect, so I picked them up from their homes and dropped them off at the Town Hall, starting with the one who lived furthest away from the Town Hall. After the concert, which was a huge success, our instructions were to collect our original charges and take them back home, so there we all were at about 9.30pm with our cars waiting for our passengers. Out trooped all these pensioners, happy and laughing, having been given tea and biscuits during the interval, waiting to be taken back home. It wasn't until then that I realised how much one elderly lady looks like another! Despite everything I did to check, I couldn't be absolutely sure which elderly lady was my original passenger so when I thought I recognised one I asked her if I was the man who drove her here and she assured me that I was. I then approached two more ladies who looked vaguely familiar who both agreed that they were the ones I originally picked up and thus I set off with my three charges, all happily chatting away to each other about how wonderful the evening had been and how lovely it was to have a nice young man to take them home! Obviously the first house I went to was the last house I had collected from and I duly pulled up and jumped out of the car to open the door for my first lady to alight. Unfortunately all three of them said "But I don't live here" and it was then that I realised I had three completely different ladies from those I had collected! Just as one elderly lady looked like another I guess to them one young man looked just like another so when I asked if I was the person who brought them they readily agreed. Fortunately they did all know where they lived, albeit miles apart, and I did eventually get them all home and they were very happy to have something else to talk and laugh about. This type of event wasn't unique to Sittingbourne Table, as I found out when I transferred to Area 12 (North Wessex), where Warminster and District Table put on an Annual Variety Show for senior citizens. The difference here was that the majority of the acts throughout the evening were performed by members of Round Table, 41 Club, Ladies Circle and Tangent.

I transferred to Mendip Round Table in Area 12 in 1977 and at one of my early meetings it was announced

Sittingbourne Round Table 1977. My good friend Ron Peak is left of me (looking at the picture) and Cliff Jones to my right. John House is Chairman (centre), Neville Huxtable is vice Chairman and John Frewin is next to him.

that Mendip was to enter the first Chew Valley Bed Race, as detailed earlier in this book, my first fund raising event with Mendip. I settled well into Mendip Round Table, joining in their regular fund raising and social service activities such as the Christmas food parcels. The idea was that we would collect food – preferably non- perishables like tins – from perceived affluent communities within our catchment area and redistribute the proceeds to individuals or families that might not be so well off, the names and addresses of whom were given to us by Social Services. This would be done just before Christmas to try and ensure those less well off would have a better time than they might have otherwise enjoyed.

We were split into areas and our first job was to distribute leaflets door to door announcing what we were trying to do and explaining to the recipients that we would call on an appointed day usually about five days hence and collect any food they were prepared to give. This time delay was to try and ensure they would have carried out the weekly shopping by the time we arrived and have some spare food. On the designated day we would then go round to where the leaflets had been distributed, knock on the doors and ask for food. The responses varied greatly. Obviously the best responses were those houses that had read the leaflet, thought we were doing a great job and readily gave food

– the best people even had their bags already packed. The worst responses were those who thought the world was full of scroungers, that they were as deserving as anybody to receive help and who wanted a full blown debate on the subject. Some people were just plain rude to us, but we had to just put on a brave face and thank them for their time and move on. Occasionally the door would be answered by an older person and unless they insisted on making a donation we would apologise for troubling them and wish them a happy Christmas. Generally we would reckon on about a 50% success rate. I remember calling at one house to be greeted by a small female who looked about 15 years old. When I asked if her mum was in she looked a bit taken aback and said her mother didn't live there. This took me a little by surprise and I was beginning to feel sorry for this little girl who had lost her mummy in circumstances that I could only imagine. I then explained who I was and what we were doing and was about to ask if I could speak to the person who was in charge of the household when a little girl ran out asking "what does the man want mummy?" Fortunately the older female saw the funny side and was a little flattered that I thought her so young, and gave us some tins for the collection.

All the food was taken to a central location – usually the Chairman of community services house – and stored in their garage until all collections were completed. His wife would usually be in attendance to give us coffee and mince pies and stories would be swapped about the collections. The food would then be sorted into boxes each containing similar items and then resorted into food hampers with the contents being dependant on whether the recipient was an individual or a family. About a week before Christmas we were given names and addresses of people who were deemed suitable to receive the hampers and they were then distributed. Again, the responses were mixed. In the main the people who received them were very grateful and obviously would benefit by the generosity of the community at large and we came away feeling good about life and people and grateful for what we had ourselves. There were occasions, however, when it seemed that Social Services had got it wrong as there were several times when Tablers came back saying they were asked to put the parcel in the main room, where there was a TV much larger than we had with furniture in better condition than we sat on. But as I say, overall we felt the event was worthwhile and it carried on for many years.

Before I joined Mendip Round Table my predecessors had undertaken a similar venture, collecting logs for open fires or log-burning stoves and distributing them amongst those in the community deemed to be most in need of such help.

Then on 23rd November 1980, three years after I joined Mendip there was a world event that was to give me one of my biggest adventures in Table. On that day an earthquake struck Southern Italy, killing more than 3,000 people. The casualty toll was so high in part because the tremor struck during Sunday night mass while many residents were sat in churches that crumbled in the quake. The 6.89-7.2-magnitude quake struck at 7:34pm on a Sunday night and was centred in Eboli, south of Naples. Over the next several weeks, it became clear that approximately 3,000 people had died and 300,000 more would be homeless as winter began. The government dispatched tents to more than 200 towns affected by the earthquake and further disaster was averted. The National Association of Round Tables immediately launched a disaster appeal, calling not only for money but for blankets, tents and even caravans for homeless survivors to live in. As our earlier members had responded to the earthquake in Skopje 17 years earlier so Mendip again launched an appeal on Friday 28th November, including TV coverage thanks to Bill Oxenham who was an editor on TV, with the object of raising money to buy a caravan. However, after a couple of days we had actually been given 7 caravans by members of the local community, including one from an individual who said he would happily drive it to the stricken area as part of any convoy that might be formed.

At this time Ian Leavey was Chairman and I received a telephone call on the "grapevine" to meet at his house on Sunday 30th November to decide how we should deal with the problem of getting to Italy the seven caravans we had accumulated. After a very short meeting we had decided that we would take the caravans down to Southern Italy ourselves and six Tablers volunteered to be the drivers, these being Ian, me, Jeff Douce, Roger Fielder, Peter Broughton and Rod O'Dare (sadly now deceased). We had other people who weren't in Round Table who volunteered to drive, two of whom later joined Table, Bob Bardle and Jon Andrewes and altogether 15 of us set off on 3 December. I had never driven on the Continent before, I had never towed a caravan and I had never driven on the Continent pulling a caravan in snow, so it really was a leap of faith for me to volunteer to be one of the drivers! I like to think I contributed to the feeling of adventure by turning up for the off in a summer "beaney" hat - but it was a Round Table standard issue hat!

One of the drivers who had no time to join Table was Barny Lovell's son Mark, who was then currently a works Rally Driver for Ford UK, who drove one of the vehicles loaned to us by Passey & Porter, Ford distributor in Weston. This was a heavily modified Range Rover (very quick), which we used like a sheep dog to round up the vehicles on the way down to Italy as they were at times separated by anything up to 10 miles apart. Sadly Mark died in May 2004 aged just 43 whilst rallying in America.

Our destination was L'Aquila, which was the nearest town to the disaster area we were told by the authorities we were allowed to drive to in Italy, where there was to be a collection point for all the caravans and other non-perishables that were donated. Unfortunately 29 years later L'Aquila itself was to be the centre of yet another earthquake tragedy for Italy. Our journey was at the beginning of winter and we had to cross mountains to reach our destination. We also put blankets in the caravans that were also needed as part of the relief requirements. A team of fund-raisers was set up amongst the remaining members of Mendip Round Table and by the time we were ready to go we had been loaned a number of 4-wheel drive vehicles to pull the vans, including a Land Rover that was to become my home for a week. Fund raising continued, which meant that all the petrol needed for the journey for the various vehicles involved was paid for and eventually we raised over £5,000.

Before we left for Italy, as we were going into an earthquake zone we all had to have various inoculations (typhoid etc). The good doctor in Axbridge was called out on his day off to give us these shots and to say he was not a happy man was an understatement. When

asked as to why he was so particularly unhappy his reply
was that all the shots he was giving us were a complete
waste of time, as they wouldn't have time to work. The
only consolation was that "although you will still get
whatever disease is going the only difference is that you
won't get it quite as bad as people in the quake zone!"

As previously explained, although Round Table as we
know it is centred in the UK it is an international
organization with clubs throughout the world, and our
organization got busy making use of our friends in
France, the first country we would visit. We were to
drive to Dover and catch the ferry to Calais, where it
was arranged we could sleep in the ferry car park, which
wasn't normally allowed. To our Calais friends this

Setting out from the Penscot Hotel

didn't seem as bad as it sounded, as they assumed we would be able to sleep in the caravans en route, but all our vans had been fumigated and were thus uninhabitable all the time we were transporting them. We therefore slept very coldly and uncomfortably in the towing vehicles in Calais car park. However, this was more than compensated for by our next stop, Dijon in Central/Southern France. Our arranged accommodation was the comfort of a Youth Hostel and we were given a Mayoral reception at a local hotel and wined and dined exceedingly well. We were also given special consular passes so that we did not have to pay the motorway tolls in France and Italy

The next day was to be the hardest day, with a drive across the mountains, stopping for food and then carrying on to L'Aquila. We were advised to have our best drivers on the mountains and, as I didn't consider myself to be one of those I volunteered to take the first shift, ready to be told when to change. Due to many circumstances, it transpired that I was to drive for 8 hours solid and when we eventually stopped I found out that I had also driven over the hardest part of the route – no longer was I a novice driver! Even more surprising was that when we stopped for food the people in the restaurant found it hard to believe we had come from Dijon, as all the reports were that the roads were impassable.

We then set off for L'Aquila, which meant going through the town of Aosta, which is where we had one of the funniest occurrences of the journey. We had become detached from a couple of the vans but there were still four vans in convoy and we came to a T junction where we wanted to turn right, with an Italian policeman on point duty. Our vans were stopped by the policeman before we could turn right and we were first in the queue. Both lanes to our right were completely clear when the policeman let us through and the lead van had a mental blockage and turned right into the left hand lane (as he would do in the UK) and not the right hand lane, with the rest of the convoy following him like sheep. By now both lanes had traffic in them and there was the sight of four caravans going down the wrong way with traffic hurtling towards us – PANDEMONIUM! Instead of sorting it out the traffic policeman stayed on his podium and left it to the Van passengers to sort out the mess, which we did, but we then realized we should have turned left at the T junction and thus we were going in the wrong direction. Somehow or other we turned the vans round and the lead van was now the one that I was in. As we came back up the road to where the policeman was stationed at the T junction I decided that I would get out and ask him the way. So we stopped about 30 metres short of the policeman and I got out of the van and started to walk towards him. At the sight of me the policeman got off his podium and started to walk away and so I started to run after him. He then broke into a trot and got faster and faster and there is this picture of a tall Englishman chasing a rather short policeman along the roads of Aosta! After a while it became obvious he didn't want to be caught so I gave up chasing him and went back to the van where we decided we would take our chances on the right direction.

I am grateful to Peter Broughton who reminded me of the following incidents en route. "When we started on the main route down through Italy as we came to toll booths it became quite clear who had family in the quake zone and who did not. As we approached a toll booth on the motorway sometimes a collector would come out and wave the rest of the traffic out the way to let us through but others were not so charitable. There was one classic incident involving Eddie who was the lead caravan as we came to one booth. He stopped but the collector refused to accept that our consular passes, even though in French and Italian, entitled us clear passage. Dear Eddie was arguing the toss and getting nowhere with the rest of the caravans piling up behind. So Mark Lovell said push him on through the toll, so guess what, that's exactly what we did giving the toll collector the well know British bird as we all went through the toll.

Further on down we came upon the French Red Cross in one of the motorway lay-bys so we stopped to let the convoy catch up. Well, Rod O'Dare and his co-driver where able to use their caravan as it had not been fumigated, but us poor lot couldn't, so when the French offered us some coffee (at this point this was pure heaven) Rod and his co-driver came out with very small cups to receive the black coffee. However to this day we have no idea what was in the coffee as one minute we were DEAD the next we were like spring chickens. The sequel to this was as we were arriving in L'Aquila quite a few hours later and were trying to find the collection/meeting point all of us who had the French coffee found that none of us could speak. When we tried to converse all our words came out jumbled. Fortunately this did not last for too long."

The only other adventure we had was when the police were called to a petrol station where we stopped to fill up. The cashier tried to rip off Roger Fielder but Jeff was having none of it and, quite rightly asked for the correct money to be returned. The cashier started arguing and out of the blue a policeman appeared. I'm not sure how but it all got sorted without us going to jail and we did get our money back, but it did leave a nasty taste in our mouth, particularly as we were on a mercy mission for their fellow countrymen. It brought home to us the divide there is in Italy between the

North and the South – the Northern Italians seemed at a loss as to why we would go out of our way to help the Southern Italians. We therefore decided that we would go to L'Aquila, drop off the caravans and head straight back home. When we eventually reached L'Aqila we were given an unqualified assurance that both the caravans and their contents were desperately needed and would be used. Having dropped off the caravans we had a really good night back in a hotel in Aosta (we didn't see our friendly policeman again!) and then set off for home.

Again I am grateful to Peter Broughton for further recollections: "One memory that stands out at the meeting point was that the warehouses were stuffed full of cloths/blankets etc. They needed sorting so the Italian Government had loaned us a couple of soldiers but these two soldiers to be kind were not a happy pair. They really didn't want to do any work or help at all, that is until someone - I can't remember who it was but is was a Tabler - came down the path and literally gave this pair a boot up their backsides with the words "Come on you lazy B......s get a move on". It really was just like a Laural and Hardy sketch. On the way back we stopped at an overnight truck stop just before leaving Italy. It was late and the only food they could offer us was toasted cheese sandwiches and wine. Well I think there were 12 of us, so by the time we had eaten and drunk enough there were quite a few empty bottles of red wine on the table. The wine was really superb and the interesting fact was that Ian or Jeff noticed as the empty bottles were lined up on the table, (quite a number I can't remember how many bottles) but the first bottle was dated something like 1969 going all the way to the present time. The last bottle tasted as good as the first."

The Land Rover I was in developed an engine fault, (a valve burnt out). It wasn't until we gave it back at home that we discovered this particular machine had always had this problem and that they were not at all surprised the valve had gone again. However it did mean that although it could be driven the maximum speed was 40 mph, which in turn meant it was a very long and slow journey home. I was by now co-driving with a guy called Mark, who was a mechanic and so delegated to help me nurse the car home, and I remember we gave a lift to two Italian soldiers who were late back to barracks from a weekend pass. We conversed with them in pigeon French as they didn't speak English and the only Italian I knew was "Come ti chiami" (what is your name?) that I had learned from our Italian neighbours when I lived with my parents in a block of flats in London!

We dropped off the soldiers and continued our journey home, stopping off at Auxerre. We stayed in a really old fashioned hotel and when we went to our rooms we were accompanied by a porter who looked about 100 years old. He beckoned us to get in a really decrepit lift to about the fourth floor while he took our cases. Although the lift was slow we were still amazed to find him waiting for us at the top of the stairs. Next morning we had one of those lovely moments that can't be replicated. Peter, Ian Leavey, Jeff Douce and I left the hotel for a short walk. We hadn't been going long when all of a sudden a big trap door opened up in the pavement along side us and next thing we know we are being handed baskets and baskets of fresh bread with the words "vite, vite (get a move on)". So there we were pulling the baskets up from the cellar into the shop. Needless to say we just had to purchase some of the wares as the smell of the freshly baked bread had been driving us wild whilst we were doing our (unpaid!) work.

The sea crossing back was pretty rough – not surprising as it was December – with many people being sea sick. Peter Broughton suggested that we had a fry-up before we disembarked and we were a little surprised to find there were only a handful of people with us in the dining room. We eventually got home on the morning of 9 December to be greeted in Dover by a customs man who told us that John Lennon had been shot dead the night before. I arrived home at 4.00am absolutely shattered and was mighty glad to see my wife and children, but it was an experience I will never forget. A couple of the caravan drivers had the foresight to leave their name and address in the caravan they delivered, and some time later one of them (I forget who) received a touching letter from a family who had been given a van, thanking them for their generosity.

Mendip Table in my day also tried to make use of the natural attraction that was Cheddar Gorge to raise funds. In a small community like ours, you did not want to always be asking for money from the local people, effectively always asking the same people to donate, so ways were thought of to raise money from tourists. One of the ways we used was to try and create a "mile of coins". The idea was that we would start at the bottom of the Gorge and ask tourists to lay coins on the pavement in a line leading up the Gorge, with the ultimate ambition of having a mile of coins. I have fond memories of Martin Bull greeting unsuspecting tourists who had crossed over the road to our side where the coins were with the words "Thank you SO much for crossing the road to add to our mile of coins!" When the tourist looked puzzled, Martin had them hooked by explaining what we were trying to achieve for charity and very few had the nerve to refuse. To avoid the possibility of anybody taking the coins, as soon as we had thirty metres or so of coins laid out we sticky-taped them to the ground. We did this for a couple of years, usually over a Bank Holiday and whilst we never raised a huge amount of money there were no overheads and it involved very little organisation on our part.

Another big earner for our charity funds was the teddy bear stall. This was introduced by Peter Smith and was a very simple but effective way of raising charity money, although it did involve an initial outlay by Mendip Round Table. The idea was that we would purchase a number of teddy bears in various sizes and colours. Peter is absolutely brilliant at making things and he made a transportable stall on which to display the teddy bears. We would take it in turns to go to various fetes and functions and sell tombola type tickets to the general public for them to try and win a bear. The idea was brilliant in that the audience for people wanting to win a bear was huge; not only would children or their parents want to enter but young men would try and win one for their girl-friends. We went to most local events where there were people and other stalls – a fete in Cheshire Homes grounds, school fetes and village fetes. Obviously the bigger the event the more tickets we sold but the beauty was that any un-won stock would be carried over to the next fete and if more stock was needed then we would merely order some more and go through the same process. In my opinion undoubtedly the best event we attended with our bear stall was the Bath Mardi-Gras, a huge attraction that brought in thousands of people. Not only was it great fun actually being on the stall but we also got to go round the other attractions when our stint was finished. I would like to record my personal thanks to Pete Smith for initiating the event, for giving me so much fun in raising money and for all his hard work he put into making the stall. Over the time we did this event we made thousands of pounds.

Just round the corner from the Gorge was the local caravan and camping site owned by the family of one of our members, David Moore. David now no longer owns it but in the latter years it became a very large concern with many attractions. In the early years, however, although it had very good bar facilities there wasn't much entertainment each day and so every Wednesday Round Table would run bingo sessions. This involved David putting up notices around the camp to attract punters and when they were in the bar we would sell bingo cards for cash to those who wanted to play. We would generally sell two games at a time using different colour printed bingo cards and the prize money depended on the number of people playing and therefore the amount of tickets purchased. As a young man one of Martin Bull's earliest jobs was selling cottons to the "rag trade" and as a result he knew the name of every colour under the rainbow; he caused a mixture of mirth and consternation when announcing, for example, that the first of the two games sold would be on the vermillion coloured bingo card, as very few people actually knew what colour vermillion was!

There was a regular band of Tablers that turned up every week and we all took turns to be the caller. We purchased a hand driven bingo ball selector that one member would operate whilst another called out the number on the balls. The holiday-makers would play with a small prize for the first line to be called out and then a larger prize for the full house, with us giving them cash prizes. We gave back a proportion of the takings as prize money with RT putting the balance into our charity account. We would always be at pains to point out that all the residual proceeds after giving out the prize money went to charity and no one ever complained to David or us. Indeed, we tried to make it as much fun as possible, with some of us interspersing the calls with jokes, and I believe Dave did actually get compliments from the holiday-makers about the bingo he put on, with many returning customers greeting us each year like long lost friends. Bingo continued for many years and it is interesting to note from the minutes of the 1989 AGM that it was more cost effective than the Teddy Bear stall, which would be reflected in the next year's efforts.

Also within our area was a local Cheshire Home, provided by the Leonard Cheshire Disability UK Services, which claims to be the UK's largest voluntary sector provider of services to disabled people. Mendip Round Table got involved with this charity in many ways, but in my time by far the greatest support we gave was time. Our biggest commitment was providing a weekly rota at the local swimming pool, in Churchill Community School to enable Cheshire Home residents to go swimming. Staff at the Cheshire Home would bring a number of residents to the school in their mini bus, but if a driver could not be found then a Mendip Tabler would also drive the bus. Tablers would assist the Cheshire Home staff in helping the male members to change into their swimming costumes; we would then lift them into the swimming pool and support them while they splashed around in the pool. At the end of their session we would lift them out of the pool, help dry them and get them dressed. It has to be remembered that in those days there was no such thing as CRB (Criminal Records Bureau) checking, which made what we were doing a lot more viable. One of our most memorable residents was a guy called Eric, a heavy chap with a broad Somerset accent who spoke very loudly. His comments were not only a source of great amusement to everybody but he made it a joy for all of us to carry out our commitments with his enthusiasm and gratitude for what we were doing for him. I don't think I will ever forget him saying – very loudly in his broad accent – "You lovely people make me laugh so much" usually two or three times each session.

We were all greatly aware of the enjoyment our efforts gave to the residents and it inspired us to use some of the money raised from our fund-raising efforts to buy a pool-side hoist that could be used by the school for all disabled people, not just when we were there with Cheshire Home residents. Also, one of our lasting legacies was to build a wheel-chair ramp for easier access to the swimming pool. As a separate event, we also took a number of residents for a day away in conjunction with the official staff, to Budeley Safari Park and indeed Colin Graves drove one of the mini buses, specially converted to accommodate wheel chairs. Once there we each assumed responsibility for one of the residents, pushing them around in their wheelchairs, and ensuring they got safely back to the mini bus ready for the trip home.

There was another community event that we got involved in called Garden Renovation Old People Exercise, or GROPE for short. This involved in identifying older folk who had gardens that they had difficulty in maintaining themselves. Members of Table would then offer to tidy up their garden and, on occasions, go back a while later and do the same again. The flaw in our plan was that this was not meant to be an ongoing commitment for ever more. Most older people realised this and were grateful for any help they received (and indeed the company they got for an afternoon) and the scheme worked well. However, there was one elderly lady who misunderstood the situation and every time she saw the member who initially tidied up her garden, Bob Hughes, she would get onto him and ask when he was coming back again to do her garden. This happened wherever he was – in the shops, in the street or even on one occasion while Bob was in a traffic jam, there was no escape for him. Again, however, in general the exercise was well worth doing.

One of our most successful fund raising events during my time in Mendip Table was the Swimarathon. It took a fair bit of organizing before the event, but was fairly easy to manage on the day. Various organizations were contacted and invited to enter teams of four to compete in a "swimarathon". All teams had to raise sponsorship money that went into Mendip Table's Charity funds and we took over Churchill Swimming Pool for an evening. Each team that participated was given a specific length of time in which to complete as many lengths as possible in the form of a relay race. There were six lanes of teams and if there were, say, 18 teams in total we would run the race three times. There were various overall prizes with each team competing for a prize in their own specific category (e.g. an age group) based on the total number of lengths completed, highest team sponsorship and highest individual sponsorship, with Tablers being the lap recorders and judges. The event would have been organised with a specific charity in mind and each team was invited to raise funds for the chosen charity using sponsorship forms provided by Mendip Round Table. Generally speaking these were a huge success and would invariably be the largest fund raising event of the year. By 1992 it was still a major event for Mendip Table and it had grown such that the event started at 12.00 noon on a Saturday in December and went on until 10.00pm. The format was that each team would consist of six swimmers and a non-swimming captain, with each team being required to swim for a total period of 45 minutes, starting on the hour. For that year the money collected was donated to CLIC (Cancer and Leukemia in Children), a favoured charity of our Table after the help that organization had given to one of our members whose daughter tragically died of that terrible disease.

An unusual, but very successful fund raising event was very much due to the good nature of the manager of our local Country Club, the Cadbury Country Club at Congresbury, bordering Yatton. At the time the manager was a guy called Trevor Joyner who had a soft spot for Round Table. He would regularly put on cabaret nights at his club with big names as top of the bill, for example the late great Roy Castle. I recall meeting Roy with David Brown, our fund raising Chairman for that year, and giving Roy the low-down on local events and characters for him to use in his act. Mendip Table was allocated a number of tickets to sell for Trevor's big nights in exchange for which he would make a generous donation to our charity funds. Generally speaking the only tickets we would sell would be for our own personal use but I remember Jeff Douce and I standing in Weston-super-Mare High Street trying to sell tickets to the general public, until we were moved on by a sympathetic but conscientious policeman, as we had no selling license or any reason for parking our car in a pedestrian precinct. I'm not sure if we ever sold our allocated number of tickets, but this didn't seem to make any difference, as Trevor still managed to sell out and make the same donation to our charity fund regardless. Trevor was also good friends to a number of us away from these events, as he would often let us into his club for a late night drink on our way back from another event, even though we weren't members, and I have very fond memories of his hospitality.

When I was Round Table Chairman I participated in what was probably the most enjoyable fund raising event of my Table career, with the only draw-back being that the very nature of it precluded my family from being there. My year in the Chair was to coincide with the 25th anniversary of the formation of Mendip Round Table and the 10th anniversary of our twinning with Cholet Round Table in France in the Loire Valley.

Obviously these events needed to be celebrated and arrangements have to be made well in advance. The Chairman when I was Vice Chairman, Peter Smith, had suggested that during my year as Chairman we undertake a bike ride from Shipham, where our Table now met, to Cholet and at the same time make it a charitable event and raise funds for Weston Hospital Radio. However this was not to be undertaken on an ordinary bike, but a six man bike – one behind the other! I have to say that initially I was sceptical as to the viability of such a project and also as to whether our members would be in favour of it. Fortunately for us, and me as Chairman in particular, Peter's enthusiasm for the project came across and it was voted for unanimously. Peter was one of the most enthusiastic Tablers I have ever met and we owe him a great debt of gratitude for all that he did in Round Table but in particular for suggesting and initially organising this wonderful adventure.

It takes a great deal of practice and training to master a six man bike and although the ride wasn't to take place until May/June we had to train for it starting in January. Unfortunately in the November before the training was due to start I developed an abscess on my backside and I was admitted to hospital for an operation. I was never convinced that the operation was successful, which proved correct as I was back in hospital a fortnight later to have another operation on the same place. I had an open wound that needed daily dressing (too much information I know, but relevant) and altogether I was off and on work for about a month. The wound takes time to heal and having a hole in your bum is not the best preparation for a bike ride! I caused a great deal of mirth when I turned up for my first practice session carrying a cushion to put on the saddle that I would be occupying.

The six man bike had been commissioned by Goodmays Round Table, and was occasionally available for use by organisations for charitable events. Goodmays Round Table had two members who were senior in their companies, one for BMW Motorbikes and the other a tubular steel firm. As already said, it was a bike that was designed to seat six riders, one behind the other. It had a BMW motorbike front and rear and a custom-built middle section made by the tubular steel company. Each rider had a set of handlebars, which was attached to the back of the saddle of the rider in front of him. Each rider had their own set of peddles, which were offset so that when everyone pushed off together you wouldn't fall over, and although it wasn't a "fixed wheel" everyone had to free wheel at the same time or none at all, there was no individual choice. It weighed around 500lb (about 227 kgs) unladen and had no gears. Thus if you had six men on it that averaged around 12 stone you had a total weight of around 1500lb or about 2/3rds of a ton, a lot of weight to move without any gears.

We had established an approximate list of those people likely to go on the trip to Cholet, although many others wanted to have a go at riding it, but we found only two guys who could actually steer it, Peter Smith and Jon Andrewes. I don't know if it was strength or technique or both (there was certainly general technique needed to keep the thing going) but unless one of these two men were at the front we couldn't get going at all. It also became traditional for Martin Bull to be anchorman whenever he was on the bike, although this position wasn't nearly so difficult to master. We had a trailer on which we could drive it to our practice area, which we decided would be Weston sea front, as it was fairly long and straight. Thus we completed our training and got used to starting, stopping and going round corners. To start, the man at the back had to keep his feet on the ground while all the others sat with feet on peddles. We then all pushed off on our individual peddles and the anchorman would run along the first few steps and then jump on his saddle and join us peddling. We all had to stop at the same time and preferably all put our feet on the floor together, all this being done on the orders of the front man.

So it was that in April 1985 I took up the position of Chairman of Mendip Round Table and in June of that year we set off on the great bike ride. There was a ten man team, Tony Fowles, Chris Wardman, Jim Ramadan, Jon Andrewes, Bob Bardle, Philip Knowles, Mike Peel, Peter Smith, Martin Bull and me. There would be six on the bike with the other four as back up in the van, with two/four hour shifts on the bike. Shipham to Cholet is a long way and bearing in mind we all worked and would have to take time off work to do the deed we decided we would make it as easy for ourselves as possible. Thus we decided to cycle from Shipham to Weymouth on a Saturday using as many Tablers as wanted to take part, load up the bike and bring it back. On the way to Weymouth a part of the bike sheared off just outside Dorchester and we had to find a garage that could help us. Fortunately the fact that it was such an amazing, unique and therefore interesting machine helped, as a chap who was about to close up his garage agreed to do some welding for us. My recollection is that it might have been FA Cup Final day, and if that was the case the chap who helped was particularly generous with his time as he was anxious to get home to watch it. Having had the repairs carried out we completed our journey to Weymouth, put the bike back on the trailer and went home.

Then the following Wednesday we loaded up the bike on the trailer again and drove it down to Weymouth where we were to get the ferry over to St Malo from whence the main team would cycle to Cholet. So that we could say that we cycled all the way, we took with us an exercise bike and took it in turns to ride the exercise bike on the ferry on the crossing. As it turned out it was a stroke of genius that we took the exercise bike, as it came in handy for spare parts.

We were to have two overnight stops in Youth Hostels and arrive in Cholet on the Friday, disperse to our French hosts and then on Saturday we would meet up with the other Tablers and wives who had not taken part in the bike ride but who wanted to attend the twin meeting anyway. The first night we spent in Dinan, a beautiful old walled town in Brittany, and from there our next scheduled stop was in Rennes. It is amazing how quickly one can get fit in necessity. Although we had trained for the event and were relatively young, none of us had done intensive training and at the end of the first day of the actual bike ride in France we were all tired and woke up stiff the next morning. However, once back on the bike the stiffness went and all of us took our prescribed turns at riding. It turned out that having no gears was the hardest part as we had only sheer brute force to get us up the hills, but it was testimony to us all that not once did we have to get off and push. This was in contrast to the ride from Shipham to Weymouth, where one set of riders repeatedly had to push up hills. Such was our fitness (and our over-cautious faith in our cycling prowess) that we actually got to Rennes early afternoon and rather than waste the rest of the day we decided to carry on cycling for a couple of hours, load the bike on the trailer and then take it back to our hostel in Rennes. The next morning we took the bike back to where we had stopped the previous afternoon and resumed our ride to Cholet from there. As the distance from Rennes to Cholet is about 100 miles we did exactly the right thing in continuing cycling the previous day, as we arrived in Cholet at exactly our expected time and on the road from Rennes to Nantes we were overtaken by our Mendip Tabler friends in their cars on their way to Cholet.

We had a really enjoyable ride through the French countryside; the French are great cyclists and were enthralled by our six man bike. We had one moment of panic that actually ended up in great hilarity. I was not on the bike at the time but was one of the team waiting at the top of a hill to provide sustenance to the riders when they eventually arrived. We could see the bike approaching, all riders out of their saddles with the strain, and at the brow of the hill we saw Tony Fowles suddenly keel over and fall off, obviously bringing all the others down with him. Tony is a big guy, slightly older then the rest of us and had taken over on the bike on the afternoon shift having had a substantial lunch, including the best part of a bottle of wine, and the first thoughts of the support team were that he had had a heart attack. We ran over to the riding team who by now were clambering to their feet to realise that Tony was lying on his back roaring with laughter. It turned out that he had put so much strain on the handlebars going up the hill out of the saddle that he had sheered them off with his strength, which obviously caused the whole team to be unbalanced and fall off. Thanks to the exercise bike we were able to replace the handlebars and carry on the journey.

When we got to the outskirts of Cholet, about 3.00pm on Friday, we telephoned the Chairman and were collected and dispatched to our various hosts to settle in for the evening. The next day we took the bike back on the trailer to the outskirts of Cholet and were escorted to the Town Hall so that everyone could meet us. Such was the influence that certain Cholet Tablers had that they had arranged for a section of road to be clear of traffic and a virtual police escort into the town. When we arrived at the Town Hall there was a wedding ceremony taking place. Unfortunately for the bride our bike became the centre of attention and everyone in the square, including the wedding guests, left the party to come and inspect our bike and ask numerous questions. I was then asked to give an interview for French radio, but I quickly declined and got Jim Ramadan to take it on as he was relatively fluent in French. Jim's wife was a French translator and I had asked her to translate from English to French a speech that I was to give at a dinner later that evening. After the radio interview I was then presented to the Cholet Mayor and I took the bull by the horns and decided I should make the speech, using some of my evening speech to respond to the mayor's welcome. I adapted the speech by presenting him with a T shirt that we had had commissioned for the occasion depicting on the front of the T shirt our six-man bike and riders.

We had all been allocated to stay with the families of Cholet Round Table and I was lucky enough to be assigned to Luc and Helene Gilbert, who had two sons (one called Yan, the same age as my son, Mathew) and a schnauzer dog with three legs. It was from this stay that we arranged an informal exchange, whereby Mathew went to stay in France at Luc's house with Yan and then Yan came and stayed at our house with

Arriving at Cholet, Jon Andrewes steering, Tony Fowles, Peter Smith, me, Mike Peel and Martin Bull at the rear

Mathew. Yet another example of the great things that can happen when you get involved with Round Table. After the Mayoral reception, in the afternoon we had a garden party for everyone, where the French Tablers presented us with bottles of wine that were bottled from a huge barrel whilst we were at the party. I have this abiding memory of sitting in the shade of a tree with Rod O'Dare, a few other Tablers and at least one of our French hosts, a guy called "Guy" (pronounced "Gee", with a hard "G"). It was mid afternoon, the sun was shining, we had had a good supply of wine, we were all feeling very relaxed and Rod was smoking his pipe (which he swore he did only to keep the flies away). From this semi-comatose state I heard Rod suddenly utter very slowly in a very English accent: "Guy old boy. In England at about 4.00 in the afternoon we have what we call "tea". Any chances of a cuppa old chap?" Obviously Guy had no idea what Rod was on about but about fifteen minutes later Rod did get his cup of tea.

In the evening of our arrival we had a dinner dance, where as Chairman I was expected to make a speech in French. I had drafted the speech in English and had it translated by Jim Ramadan's wife into French and over the weeks leading up to the trip had been practising it, but I was still nervous standing up in front of 100 or so people when the time came for me to deliver. The speech wasn't very long and was going reasonably well when some of the French guests started laughing at a point where there wasn't meant to be a joke. However, I took this as a good sign, finished the speech, received the response from the French Chairman and we had a good evening dancing. At breakfast next morning I mentioned to Luc that people had laughed at an inappropriate time during the speech, and he asked me what I had intended to say. I explained that in the speech I had meant to say "Since we have been in your country we have had many exciting times". Luc explained that what I had actually said was "Since we have been in your country we have had many climaxes"! It was hardly surprising that the French had found this funny.

The rest of the trip went off very well, with the highlight probably being Martin Bull standing on two chairs (one foot on each chair) in a café telling "un fable au sujet d'un petite oiseau" (a story or joke about a small bird) to the assembled congregation that included French and English Tablers, plus a few ordinary café customers, in "Franglais" – a mixture of French and English. How he pulled it off I don't know but everyone understood exactly what he was talking about and at the end he got a standing ovation. As a memento of our trip all the cyclists were presented with a glass replica of the bike. This has pride of place in our glass cabinet and I would be heartbroken if anything were to happen to it.

There was a sequel to the story that I feel is worth telling. We raised a considerable sum of money for

Weston Hospital Radio and it was arranged for me to present a cheque in Weston-super-Mare to Danny La Rue, the well known cabaret artist and female impersonator, on behalf of Weston Hospital Radio. This was to ensure we got good publicity for Round Table and was also a way of thanking all the people who had made donations. The time was set for 4.00pm for me to meet Danny, as it turned out on a hot sunny summer Saturday. At the time Philip Avery had a heard of sheep and I had agreed to help him with the annual sheep dipping, which involved catching the sheep, carrying them and putting them in the pit which contained the sheep dip and then ensuring they came out safely the other side. Naturally as the day wore on and I was handling more and more sheep I was taking on the smell of the sheep-dip. All was going well. I was to leave Philip at about 2.00pm, go home and shower, grab a bite to eat and then go into Weston. Unfortunately at about 1.45pm Philip's wife Tricia arrived at the field to say that we had been asked to bring forward the presentation to 3.00pm, which gave me an hour and a quarter to get home, shower, change and get to Weston. In normal circumstances this would seem an adequate amount of time but the smell of sheep-dip is not easy to remove. I did shower etc. and turned up almost on the stroke of 3.00pm but the shower was only a very quick one, not nearly as thorough as I had intended, and it was a rush. Mr La Rue then kept me waiting for almost an hour before meeting me during which time I was getting hotter and hotter and I was conscious that the smell of sheep-dip, which in my rush I hadn't completely cleansed from my skin, I felt was beginning to seep through my pores. I'm sure that the smell was not as bad as I imagined and indeed I am equally sure that Mr La Rue was very busy, but it did seem that our meeting was very short and to this day I don't know if the reason for that was the rather noxious fumes I felt was emanating from me.

During my time in Table I had introduced a number of men into the organisation, a number of which were as a direct or indirect result of my association with boy's football, so it was natural that over time we had a good

Me presenting Danny La Rue with the cheque for
Weston Sunshine Radio

number of Tablers that were interested in football. One of the most interested was Jeff Douce and he decided to organise a five-a-side football tournament in Axbridge. Local teams would be invited to enter for the payment of an entry fee, to compete for a cup. The money raised would be as a result of the entry fees, and as we begged or borrowed the equipment we had no real expenses. Mendip Table would provide the organisation, trophy, posts, ball and referees and the number of teams entered determined that the competition would be run on a league basis over the summer months. We had a fair team and although we didn't win the tournament we put up a good show, enjoyed ourselves and surprised a few of the locals who thought we would be a walk-over. My highlight though was not in our play but in the sometimes eccentric refereeing of our one and only qualified referee, Jim Ramadan, personified by his actions when he was refereeing one of our games. The opposition had a corner and I was in the middle of the area surrounding our goal to protect the cross. The winger kicked the ball but it stayed low. The ball hit the post and went straight back to him whereupon he trapped it and started to dribble towards me. I shouted "Free kick ref, he can't do that" [an opponent is not allowed to touch the ball twice from a corner kick without another person touching the ball] but Jim's answer was merely to wave his hands in a forward motion and shout back at me "Advantage, play on". In the grand scheme of things it really didn't matter and we had a good laugh about it afterwards, perhaps embodying the enjoyment we generally got from fund raising events.

As explained earlier, my predecessors in Round Table had gone round the local pubs to raise money for the Aberfan disaster in Wales. In my time in Mendip Round Table we did the same thing over a number of years to help raise funds for Children In Need, as featured on the BBC. The BBC website states that the BBC's first ever broadcast appeal for children was a five-minute radio broadcast on Christmas Day in 1927, raising £1,143 18s 3d which was split between 4 prominent children's charities. It goes on to say that the first televised appeal was the 1955 'Children's Hour Christmas Appeal', presented by Sooty and Harry Corbett. The Christmas Day Appeals continued on TV and radio right up until 1979, raising a total of £625,836 with the presenters including Terry Hall, Eamonn Andrews, Leslie Crowther, Michael Aspel and the rising star of the Radio 2 Breakfast Show - Terry Wogan - who made his debut appearance in 1978. In 1980 the appeal was broadcast on BBC One in a new telethon format, hosted by Terry with Sue Lawley and Esther Rantzen. To date over £600m has been raised and in the early years before the large Corporates became as involved as they are now Round Table as an organisation was one of the largest contributors to Children in Need. It still raises a considerable sum today but with membership now a lot less than it was in my day the contribution made by Round Table is not as obvious. Mendip Table did not get involved in specific organised activities like other Tables did, but we still did our bit by dressing up in fancy dress and rattling tins in the local pubs.

I have already mentioned the propensity for Mendip Table to participate in quizzes, notably with Llandridrod Wells, and indeed we took it on ourselves to organise our own quiz. Instead of limiting entry to our own Area we decided to invite all Tables with whom we had had a vague association and so it came about that we had one of our most successful fund raising events that happened annually over a number of years. Indeed, we even had Tables turn up that we had no association with; Chris Wardman was one of the organisers and he sent an invitation to the "wrong" Table in Reading, with whom we had no association whatsoever, but they turned up anyway.

As always in those days the venue was to be the Cadbury Country Club, with the original intention to have it in the smaller room near the pool, but as the number of entries increased our good friend Trevor Joyner agreed we could have it in the main room.

Unbeknown to us, but quickly sussed out by Blackwood Table, there was a party of ladies doing aerobics by the pool side. It needs to be remembered this was at a time when aerobics was in its infancy and the sight of women cavorting around in lycra was not as prevalent as it is today. As usual Blackwood were in their rugby shorts and they decided they would treat the aerobics girls to a display of men's legs and proceeded to parade round the pool. It transpired that these ladies were equally up for a laugh and during the interval of our quiz they reciprocated by coming up to our room and gave an impromptu display of aerobics to the throng of very appreciative Round Tablers. We put on the quiz for a number of years but we never quite equalled the aerobics entertainment in later ones.

There are two other fund raising/community service activities that stick out in my mind, both involving carnivals in Axbridge, albeit different types of carnival celebrations. The first of these memories is that involving the annual Blackberry Carnival where local organisations and individuals are encouraged to enter floats in a parade, with the highlight being the Carnival Queen and often a small fair in the town centre. This is memorable to me because it encapsulates the spirit of family that Mendip Round Table engendered – more of this later. We decided to enter a float but as was often the case left it until the last minute to organise anything and we were still preparing it on the morning of the carnival. In all truthfulness it wasn't a very good float but this did not detract from the day, as both my children helped in the preparation and then joined me on the float in the afternoon, happily waving to the spectators on the carnival route.

The second of my memories is the Axbridge Pageant, an event that happens once a decade and recreates the area's history from the Tudors right up to the Second World War. In 1980 Mendip Round Table held meetings at the Oak House in the centre of the town, owned by Nick Barrington whose great passion was photography and he was naturally involved with the production of the 1980 Axbridge Pageant. It followed that Mendip Round Table would be involved and various members were given assorted jobs to do. I was situated at the top of the tower of St John The Baptist Church, which is just off the town square where various scenes were being shot from ground level looking up. I was responsible for ensuring the players went on and off scenes from instructions given from the ground, but we didn't have radio controlled handsets so relied on shouted directions. When we Tablers went to charitable events we usually wore our Round Table tee shirts to distinguish us from the crowd and I thought it would be a good idea for me to wear my tee shirt so that the director could see me from below. Unfortunately however, it was too distinguishable and production had to be halted whilst something was found for me to wear over my tee shirt, as all that could be seen from below was my bright yellow tee shirt completely out of keeping with the medieval scene being shot. A cassock was found for me to wear and I certainly blended in. One of the players commented that I now looked the part and I remarked that he certainly looked like the part he was playing, a vicar. "I'm pleased about that", he replied, "as I am the vicar of this church!" Although I had only a small part to play in the production, I was very pleased to be part of what turned out to be a very successful pageant.

SPORTS

Although not everyone in Mendip Table was sport-minded the majority of Tablers were, and even those that weren't so inclined managed to derive some pleasure from the many and varied sports that were on offer over the years they had in Round Table. Whichever Table I visited, including Area meetings, whenever the Sports Officer got on his feet to give his report during a business meeting he would invariably be greeted with all the members singing the iconic tune that heralded the 5.00pm Saturday radio programme "Sports Report" that to this day is still played at that time on Radio 5 – "de dum de dum de dummidy dum, de dum de dum de dum" etc etc. Along with many other wives of Round Tablers, my wife has often said that we were all like big kids and if she had ever been at a meeting when the Sports Officer stood up to address the meeting this would surely had confirmed her thoughts. As a lover of all sports I got even more out of Round

Table because of this, but, as already stated most members got at least a modicum of enjoyment at some time or another.

As with all posts within Round Table if the officer in charge of the position was keen, enthusiastic and active then his year as Chairman of that particular function was a far greater success than if the incumbent was dull and lifeless. This was probably truer in the Fund Raising position but it is still important for the Sports Officer to be vibrant and have many ideas. We were very fortunate in Mendip Round Table to have a number of enthusiastic guys who brought different ideas each year in their time as Sports Officer.

I have already mentioned my time in Sittingbourne Round Table taking part in "Bat and Trap" and Area football matches. The Area football continued in Mendip along with cricket, rugby and Tug-O-War, as already described, but in addition to the different Area sports events thanks to our Sports Officers we did other things on our own. One of the most memorable things we did was gliding. One of our members owned his own glider and close to us at Weston-super-Mare was an airfield that had the facilities to allow us to participate in this thrilling sport. I can't recall if there was more than one session, but I do know that everyone who wanted the opportunity to go up in the glider achieved their ambition, and how fabulous was the experience. There are two methods to get a glider airborne that I know of, by being towed behind an airplane that has an engine and then releasing the "tow-rope" when the glider has reached a certain height, and the other method is to catapult the glider into the air by means of a giant winch. Winch launches are cheaper than aerotows and have the advantage that many members of a club can be taught to operate the equipment. A winch may also be used at sites where an aerotow could not operate, because of the shape of the field or because of noise restrictions. The height gained from a winch is usually less than from an aerotow so pilots need to find a source of lift soon after releasing from the cable, otherwise the flight will be short.

It was this latter method that was used for us and I was surprised by the amount of "G force" that was experienced during our assent. Once air-born the sensation is even better, just floating around with the only noise being the swoosh of the air over the wings. Obviously we had to have a qualified pilot go up with us and one of the skills of the pilot is to find the thermals to enable the glider to gain height and on a good day with a good pilot it is possible to stay in the air for many hours and to cover immense distances. Clearly for us we didn't have the time to go great distances but the views were superb and everyone had the opportunity to take over the controls during their flight. Everyone who went up came back enthusing about their flight but unfortunately it is the only time I have participated in what seems to me to be a fantastic sport.

Another sport that I would never have had a go at if it hadn't been for Round Table was pot-holing or caving as it is also known – and I think it's fair to say that having done it once I would not want to do it again. We are fortunate(?) to have many caves near where we live and indeed people come from miles around to go pot-holing in our area. This was one of those events that was organised as an alternative to a Table night and thus was well attended, complete with a prospective member who had already been to a couple of meetings and was thus obviously keen to join in our other activities. We obviously had a fully qualified guide and were told to turn up in old clothes that we wouldn't be too upset if they got too badly worn during the evening so they could never be used again. I can't remember if it was only the really clever ones amongst us that turned up in boiler suits or if we were all given them, but we quickly realised the wisdom of wearing them. We found out that in the cave it was relatively cold, dusty and damp and there was a fair degree of crawling involved. We were also given what looked like an old fashioned miner's helmet, complete with candle that had to be lit. Although this looked very antiquated it turned out to be very efficient and did light the way ahead.

Off we set, all in single file to an obvious chorus of "Hy ho, hy ho, it's off to work we go" and entered what we were told was an "easy" cave to explore. Very quickly we were on our hands and knees and then shortly after crawling on our tummies with very little space between us and the cave ceiling. The idea was that we would go along a shaft to a dead end then manoeuvre round and go back again. At the very beginning of being on my tummy I was having problems. With my hands in front of me I raised my head to see where I was going and hit my head (fortunately protected by the helmet) on the cave ceiling. The natural reaction was to lower my head very quickly, which resulted in the lamp coming into contact with the back of my hand and burning it. This in turn caused a natural reaction to quickly raise my head again, which hit the ceiling again, which caused me to lower it again quickly onto the back of my hand, which caused......After doing this rapidly about three times in succession I finally got my brain in gear, moved my hand from being directly under my head and only raised my head sufficient to see where I was going.

Eventually we all manoeuvred ourselves out of the cul-de-sac and continued our exploration of the cave, with the final exercise being to take a short leap across a chasm (with the chasm itself narrowing to a small gap about three metres below) onto a ledge, haul yourself onto the ledge through a very narrow opening and then walk along the final passage out into the fresh air. Once out we all changed and went to the local inn to have a light meal, a few pints and talk about our experiences. With very few exceptions we all agreed that we found it claustrophobic, a not very pleasant experience that we probably wouldn't repeat, but nonetheless glad that we had done it if for no other reason than to "cross it off the list" and to realise at first hand that it wasn't the sport for us.

Obviously not everyone came out of the caves at the same time and we all waited until the last people had returned and shared their experiences with the rest of us. We then realised that one of our members had not come back for the pint – our prospective member - and we were told that at the very last obstacle he had become stuck. He was in fact a little larger than the majority of us and, as I had had a little difficulty getting through some of the narrow chambers I wasn't too surprised this had happened, but was very sad that it had to be our prospective member. Even sadder was that we never saw him again; we were assured that he had been rescued but were told it had unfortunately caused him some difficulties and he had not enjoyed the experience at all. To this day I am not sure why he didn't pursue his Tabling career, but I hope it wasn't primarily due to his pot holing experience.

Also during my time with Round Table I had my first

experience of Go-Karting, which had been organised at the Clay Pigeon Raceway near Dorchester. Apart from Martin Bull, who it transpired had represented England years ago in the sport's infancy, none of us had been Go-Karting before and had no idea what to expect. While others were arriving Chris Donald took the opportunity to get in some practice and jumped in a Kart. After a couple of laps he was called in but had no idea there was no brake, so took his eye off the road to look for the brake inside and outside of the Kart. Obviously he didn't find it but in his quest for the non-existent implement he had drifted off the track and ended up in the car park. We all had a go at, what was to us, a new sport and indeed Chris showed a fair amount of talent, but it was the experience of Martin that won the day and the coveted title of top driver amongst us Tablers.

However, ask any Mendip Tabler what was THE highlight of the many sports events made available to them and they will undoubtedly all say the outward bound weekends at Plas Yr Antur in Fairbourne, North Wales. This was actually a Methodist run organisation, situated opposite and set in the outstanding scenery of the Mawddach Estuary and the Cadair Idris mountain range offering outdoor activities such as mountaineering, abseiling, canoeing etc. When we went there the warden was Bob Llewellyn who in fact eventually took it over in 1985. I actually only remember going on one trip, the inaugural trip, and I recall we set off on a Friday after I had been playing golf for most of the day with Martin Bull, getting absolutely soaking wet in the process. We rushed home and got changed and packed our gear in time to get on an old mini-bus that we had either hired or borrowed to take us the 175 miles or so to our destination, arriving fairly late at night.

The accommodation was pretty basic, with sleeping arrangements in dormitories and after a swift late meal we congregated in the main area to decide what we were going to do over the next couple of days, but particularly the next day. Obviously warden Bob knew none of us and certainly didn't know about Bob Hughes' dry wit. Bearing in mind this was due to be a weekend of high activity I think he was a little taken aback when he asked what we wanted to do on Saturday and Bob instantly replied "Well I thought we could get up about 11.00, have a bit of brunch and then wander on down to the pub......." In fairness his riposte was just as caustic and the atmosphere was set for our stay, lots of Mickey-taking and banter.

There were many activities on offer and the day was set with a gorge walk in the morning, with the alternative of pony trekking over the mountains, with rock climbing and abseiling in the afternoon. For some reason Philip Knowles and I decided to go pony trekking, which turned out to be the "wimp's option", as the gorge walk was real outdoor, manly activity stuff. Whilst Philip and I had a perfectly pleasant day, with great scenery viewing, it wasn't very strenuous and certainly didn't provide the talking points and fun that the gorge walk provoked. The gorge walk consisted of walking along a dry river gorge, but there were places where either the path was very narrow with water below whereby if you slipped you got wet, or the path was non-existent and the only way to get further along the route was to swing across on a rope, or just jump in and swim across. As most Mendip Tablers will recall, due to polio sustained as a child, Bob Hughes has a withered right arm and the fact he attempted any of these activities at all was testimony to his cussedness, and the abiding memory of the gorge walk for those that went on it was turning round to see Bob say very loudly "F**k it", throw himself in the water and swim one-armed on his back across the expanse of water in front of him.

After lunch Philip and I joined the rest of the party to attempt rock climbing and abseiling in the afternoon. The rock we were climbing was about 20 metres high, but we all had hard hats on, there was an instructor at the bottom and the top and we were roped to the top of the climb thus it was perfectly safe; if we were to slip our weight was taken by the guys at the top. That said it was still a bit scary and certainly hard work. One instructor climbed up the rock to give us an idea of what to do, without the safety of a rope, giving a running commentary as he went, and he made it look easy. This should be a piece of cake! Those who wore jeans quickly found out why the instructors had suggested we wore track suit bottoms if we had any, as jeans are not very flexible and become less so as you get hot and sweaty. The instructors also had the correct climbing shoes, and again our trainers that we wore were certainly inadequate in comparison.

They stressed that climbing was as much about the use of legs than arms, but certainly for me it did seem that my inadequacies were more in the strength of my fingers than my legs. The instructors seemed to find hand holds in the sheerest of rock and then cling by their finger-tips whilst they adjusted their feet, in one particular manoeuvre taking their whole weight on their fingers whilst swinging their legs onto another tiny ledge/rock crack. Near the top of the climb there was an option of continuing the climb straight up, or if you felt particularly adventurous you could take on a "chimney", which involved using your back and legs to navigate up a narrow chimney like hole to the top. It was impossible to tell how much free climbing you were doing and how much support you were getting from the instructor at the top, as the rope supporting you was invariably taut, but I was quite pleased with myself as I slipped only once and left semi-dangling against the rock face. However, the exertion was palpable and I was not alone in going straight to the top rather than attempting the chimney climb, as I felt I had very little strength left to do it without ending up being hauled up by the top instructor.

Once at the top we were given the option of abseiling down, which I believe we all did. Again we were roped in and allowed to abseil down at our own speed. This involved leaning out over the side of the precipice (the hardest part for most) then pushing against the rock face with your legs so that you were at an angle of about 90 degrees and then "walking" down the rock face to the bottom, feeding the rope via carabenas and then through your hands to control your descent. We were given gloves to wear to ensure we didn't get rope burns, which if we had sustained them could have meant we let go of the rope. Not that we were in any danger if this happened, as again we had the comfort of a controlling rope handled by the instructor at the top. If you had the confidence you could "jump" down instead of walking but must like me went down by the slower route. I don't have a particular fear of heights, and I found this most enjoyable.

In the evening we had a communal meal and then wandered down to the local pub, where there was nearly some unpleasantness when a couple of the local –Welsh speaking- men took a bit of umbrage to having their pub taken over by a number of loud Englishmen (and one Welshman). However, this was quickly sorted and my memory is that we ended up having a sing-song with them.

The next day was for me the highlight of the weekend and this was sea kayaking, although again it wasn't without incident. The kayaks we had were ones with an apron, thus our legs were inside the boat, along with one elongated paddle that we used to pull ourselves along by stroking with the paddle alternatively either side of the kayak. When I say "our legs", I am excluding Peter Smith who was too big to fit in the apron and had to balance precariously on top of the boat. However, before going out to sea we were taken to a quiet back-water where we could get to learn the rudiments of the sport and given instructions as to how to paddle and what to do if one of our party was to capsize. We were not given instructions as how to do an "Eskimo roll", which is where you use your paddles to refloat yourself if you do capsize, as this would take too much practice over a period of time that we didn't have. We were merely told that if we did capsize (turn upside down) we should not panic but to push down against the boat to free ourselves and then push up to the surface. We all had buoyancy aids strapped to us that fitted around our necks so there was no logical way any of us would drown if we did capsize. It was up to our colleagues to rescue our boat and paddle to make sure they didn't float away and if possible help us back into the kayak. To get as acquainted with our craft as possible, we carried out an exercise whereby we manoeuvred all our boats against each other in a line, then the one on the end of the line got out of the boat and ran along and back down the line of boats. If the boats were tightly packed together there was no danger the movement would tip them over and at the same time provide a platform stable enough for the runner. We were encouraged to use this formation if possible in event of one of us capsizing to aid the recovery of the capsized canoeist.

Following our brief practise we loaded the kayaks back on the trailers and set off for Barmouth to kayak on the sea. Once we arrived we donned our wet-suits, which was an experience in itself. Many of us had never worn a wet-suit before and our struggles to put them on were a great source of mirth for the rest of us, once again with Peter being the most difficult to clothe because of his sheer bulk. He is not a particularly fat man but at 6ft 3ins and weighing in at about 16 stone there weren't too many wet-suits around to fit him. Our trip was to take several hours, and we had been given a packed lunch to sustain us for the trip. This was tucked away in our boat by our feet (or at least that is where I put mine, along with a pair of spectacles in case I lost my contact lenses) and off we set.

The sea was fairly gentle and the tide was with us as we paddled our way along the shore line and slightly out to sea and we all gained in confidence the further distance we covered. Inevitably a couple of the guys capsized but there were enough of us around to grab the boat and paddle, turn the boat the right way up again and keep it steady enough while the guy climbed back in. After a fair time (it seemed like about an hour and a half) Bob Llewelyn signalled for us to turn round and go back to where we had left the transport when disaster struck me. Whether it was complacency or a rogue wave I don't know, but as I tried to turn the kayak round using my paddle as I had been taught I felt myself going sideways and there was nothing I could do to stop myself from turning upside down. In those situations everything seems to go into slow motion. Clearly your legs feel trapped in the boat but then you remember the instructions not to panic and to push down, which I did, and the next moment I was bobbing to the surface. Someone shouted to me to grab my boat, which was already the right way up and I managed to scramble back in whilst a couple of the guys held me steady, and then they handed the paddle back to me and we set off again, wet but no harm done and the wet-suit had done it's job and I wasn't cold. It was then that I realised the real disaster – my packed lunch which was in the well of the boat had fallen out and there was to be no lunch for me! I then also realised that I had also lost my spare spectacles, but in all honesty that paled into insignificance compared to the loss of my lunch.

Having joined up with the main party we set off back to shore. It was then we realised the tide was now against us and it was a completely different kettle of fish paddling against the tide than it had been on our outward journey. Whereas before we were paddling effortlessly and it seemed going at a good speed now we were having to work extremely hard to cover any distance at all and for long periods it seemed we were making no headway whatsoever. It also seemed the wind had picked up, and where I had got wet and wasn't covered by the wet-suit I was beginning to get a little cold. After what seemed like hours we managed to get close enough to the shore where the effect of the current seemed to have less effect and eventually we paddled onto the beach and I climbed out of the kayak, almost exhausted. I don't mind admitting there had been times when we were paddling back when I had wondered what would happen if I ran out of strength completely and was unable to beat the tide, but in the end obviously I didn't have to find out. I don't know if the other guys had struggled as much as I had done but they all looked pretty tired and on top of that poor Roger Burdock, who had also had a ducking, looked absolutely freezing as he sat shivering by the truck. I'm also pleased to report that some of the guys took pity on me and shared their lunch with me, and it's amazing how quickly your (or at least my) spirits are lifted after you have eaten. For me none of that detracted from the superb experience that sea kayaking had given me and after we had dried off and warmed up we all agreed as to what a great time we had had, again something that it is likely we wouldn't have experienced if we hadn't been in Round Table. Back at base I was presented with a badge with the inscription of "Half an Eskimo roll", which aptly describes what happens when you turn your kayak over and have to bale out.

Although I only have vivid memories of one visit, I must have been on at least one other trip, as I do remember climbing Cadair Idris and it would not have been possible to do this along with the other events already described in just one weekend visit. However, I am grateful to Chris Wardman for recounting some of the events that happened either on subsequent trips I didn't go on, or on trips on which I went but can't remember.

On one such trip Chris recalls taking a coach to Llanberis Pass, with the objective of walking up Snowdon. The route taken was not an easy route and part of the walk involved scrambling along a narrow precipice, with a sheer drop to one side. The leader Bob Llewelyn suggested that they went in single file with one competent, confident walker followed by a less competent person, then a confident one and so on, and it transpired that Roger Burdock was following David Brown. They got to a particularly hairy bit when Roger tapped David on the shoulder and said "Excuse me David. Sorry for troubling you but could you tell me, am I the competent one of us two, or is that you?!"

I don't know if it was on the same trip, but Chris also recalls going rock climbing at Llanberis, followed by an over-night stay in a cave, sleeping on the floor in sleeping bags. Whilst the cave was dry, it was a bit smelly and completely black when lights were out. If anyone had a call of nature during the night they had to clamber around/over the other guys, out of the cave and be careful not to go too far as there was a drop of some considerable magnitude not far from the cave entrance.

On another trip they set off from Fairborn along tiny roads in a mini-bus with Chris, Bob Hughes and Roger Fielder on board, when the driver Bob Llewelyn had what was virtually a head-on crash with a transit van full of workers. Unperturbed, they carried on to whatever event they were going to. Indeed it might have been another kayaking sea trip, as Chris recalls kayaking down the estuary to the coast, lunching at a disused mining village then back again accompanied by seals.

For Jim Ramadan this was a particularly gruelling return trip, as the kayak he was in developed a leak and he nearly sank by the time he got back to shore.

Later on the outward bound centre at Plas Yr Antur went out of business but Mendip Table found another centre at Morfa Bay Outdoor Centre at Pendine, Dyfed. In March 1993 a party of 34 assorted Mendip Tablers, Weston Tablers, 41 Club members and guests went on the first weekend trip to this venue.

Although generally the majority of Round Tablers can be pretty parochial and attend only their own club's events, and occasionally their Area events, there was one Area event that seemed to transcend all parochialism – "Super Fish". This event was put on by Lyme Regis Round Table, not even in our own area, but attracted Tablers from far afield. Indeed they welcomed everybody and treated it as a fund raising event and on more than one occasion I took non-Tablers as my guest to the function. In theory this event could be entered in the "Fund Raising" section of this book, but we in Mendip Table treated it as a sporting event, as it wasn't our Table's fund raising. The evening was very simple. It took place after work on a summer evening and Tablers turned up at an appointed hour on the quay side. One of our members, Bill Limbrick, didn't quite understand the travelling arrangements. It was arranged that he should be picked up en route at "seven o'clock". Unfortunately Bill thought the fishing trip was an all day event and turned up at the agreed rendezvous at "seven o'clock" in the morning and had a very long wait! Once assembled on the quay side Tablers were put in boats and taken mackerel fishing. Everyone on board was given fishing tackle (basically a line with multiple hooks on) and bait and the boatman, a very experienced man, would take us off shore where it seemed the mackerel would virtually give themselves up. After about 45 minutes fishing the boat would return to shore and the catch would be divvied up between the Tablers on board. I have fairly good sea legs (as evidenced during the return trip from Calais on the "Italian Job") but on one of the trips I had a really bad case of sea sickness. It was a very calm sea and my fishing line got tangled up with another line. We pulled the lines out of the water and instead of looking at the horizon I concentrated on untangling the lines. Wrong decision, as after ten minutes or so of such concentration I became nauseous and sick. The amazing thing was that as soon as my feet touched land again the sickness finished and I felt as god as new.

Once the catch had been divided we put our haul back in the cars and went to the Lyme Regis Powerboat Club where we were given a meal and entertainment was laid on in the form of 2 or 3 strippers. I recall upsetting one of the strippers who invited me to take off with my mouth a marshmallow she had attached to her breast, by telling her that I didn't like marshmallows, and did she have any fruit gums instead? Indeed there were stories of some men who had taken part in audience participation with the strippers and had gone home covered in baby oil. Realising their wives would be suspicious if they had a shower at 1.00 in the morning to remove the baby oil, before going to bed they smoothed a couple of mackerel over their bodies so when they went into their bedroom their wives would say "you're not coming to bed smelling like that – go and have a shower".

The whole evening was great fun and we would invariably get home at about 1.00am in the morning. I have vivid memories of dropping Terry Humberstone off at his house and him gutting all the mackerel that our car load had caught in his kitchen before we took them home. Suffice to say that Jenny his wife was not amused to come down to the kitchen next morning to be greeted by the smell of about 60 mackerel that had been cleaned in her kitchen.

SOCIAL

Recently I was discussing with Chris Wardman why we believed that Round Table was so successful during our years that we were members, and we came to the conclusion that one of the main reasons was that for us it became almost a way of life and formed the main basis of our whole social life. I'm sure that today's young men could also get the same rewards if they were to have the same approach, but nowadays there are so many more organisations for them to join that in fairness they aren't able to devote the same amount of time to one establishment such as Round Table. I also believe that today's fathers are more hands on with their children than we or certainly I was, and that their wives who are also mothers go back to work earlier than their parents did, both factors that contribute to the young men of today being less inclined to spending hours away from their families in Round Table activities. That said, whilst we got a lot out of Round Table as individuals by way of fellowship, we also got a lot out of the organisation with our wives and families through the many social functions we attended with them, organised by the Social Committee. It goes without saying therefore that this post has the potential for being the most fun to organise. However, it can also be the hardest work of all posts for the organiser and as these events still need to be prepared they obviously take time.

As the position also involves organising the annual Ladies Night, which is the most prestigious event of the year and arguably the most important night for the Chairman, the position of social secretary can also be quite nerve racking because this is the one event that you really want to be a success. Ladies Night varies in format from Table to Table but in Mendip it nearly always took place towards the end of a Chairman's year in office. It was a formal evening with the men dressed in black ties (Dinner Jackets etc) and the ladies in their best frocks, and was meant as a way of saying thank you to the wives of Tablers for all they had put up with from their husbands in the name of Round Table over the previous year. A suitable date had to be agreed, a venue had to be chosen, a menu selected and music for dancing had to be provided, preferably in the form of a live band – all within the constraints of a tight budget such that it was affordable for all, and the price of tickets didn't serve to deter the less well off Tabler from attending. There were formal speeches by way of toasts and it was traditional for the Vice Chairman to present the most important speech of the evening, the toast to the Ladies, and the Chairman of Ladies Circle would respond. Good speeches would not necessarily guarantee the evening would be a success but overlong, bad speeches meant that the rest of the entertainment had to be top drawer to prevent the evening being a poor one.

Inevitably I remember best the Ladies Night when I was Vice Chairman (and obviously also when I was Chairman). As Vice Chairman I made a speech that wasn't necessarily the best (in fact it definitely wasn't the best) but it certainly turned out to be one of the most memorable. On the basis that people like to hear their name mentioned in speeches my ploy was to mention as many Tablers as possible, even if it meant using them fictitiously in jokes, and in the main this seemed to be serving me well. But then things went wrong. I had what I thought was an undeserved reputation for being a Male Chauvinist Pig and unfortunately I didn't do much to change this opinion when I told a rather anti-female joke. Suffice it to say that one or two of the ladies threw bread roles at me. On the other hand when my wife was Chairman of Ladies Circle she got great support when she responded to the Vice Chairman's speech to the Ladies by having great courage to give half of her speech by way of a song. There was a well known old song called "A You're Adorable" (also known as the Alphabet Song) and with the help of David Brown Linda adapted the words to make it "T You're a Tabler" etc. and duly performed it in front of the whole audience. As I say that took a lot of courage and to this day I am in awe of her. The ladies got their own back on me when I was Chairman and the then Ladies Circle Chairman, Wendy Graves, responded to the Vice Chairman's speech. At the time I was losing my hair and had what I (wrongly) thought to be an un-noticeable "comb over". Wendy's speech included making "appropriate" presentations to Round Tablers and she drew attention to my comb over by presenting me with the "Bobby Charlton Award". Even non football-loving members of the audience saw the joke.

In addition to the dancing entertainment it was traditional in Mendip Table for the Tablers to put on some supplementary "amusement" for the fun of the guests in the form of a cabaret or similar activity, which usually meant dressing up, very often in women's clothes. Over the years David Brown seemed to be at the centre of Ladies Night entertainment, and continued his involvement long after I left Round Table and he even carried it on at 41 Club Ladies Nights. Taking all this into account the organisation of a good Ladies Night was no mean feat and it was very helpful if the Social Secretary had a good team behind him.

Ladies Nights at Sittingbourne followed the same format and it was attendance at my first Ladies Night that prompted me to buy my first Dinner Suit and bow tie. My background was such that I had never had cause to own such a suit and, quite rightly so it turned out, it seemed to me that it would be worth my while buying one if I was to attend such functions on a regular occurrence rather than hire them every time. Once firmly ensconced in Round Table I quickly realised there were numerous occasions during the year that such a garment would be needed and I certainly got a lot of wear out of the many dinner suits I have had since then. I wasn't in Sittingbourne Round Table long enough to enjoy many Ladies Nights but there were two that stick out in my mind.

The first one that I remember was because of the menu that was printed for the occasion. The Chairman at the time was John House, a keen footballer who had indeed represented Sittingbourne FC. In acknowledgement of this the menu was printed in the format of a football programme, with the centre pages showing all the members of Sittingbourne Round Table set out as two football teams, with those in excess of 22 being managers, referees and linesmen. The whole evening was football themed, which suited me down to the ground because of my love of football.

The other Sittingbourne Ladies Night I remember

is because of the entertainment we laid on. The Chairman Lynn Davies was fiercely Welsh, and it was his last official year in Table (although he went on to have an honorary year), having joined when he was aged 18 and had been through the Chair once already. In all he did 34 years in Table and was as enthusiastic in his last year as he was in his first. I have never known anyone else who came anywhere near giving as much length of service to Round Table as he did. As a tribute to Lynn we other Tablers secretly met up in various houses and rehearsed "We'll Keep A Welcome" which we sang at Ladies Night. We rehearsed for weeks and Lynn had no idea we were doing it. On the night we were perfect, we all knew the words and our harmonies were spot on, and Lynn had tears in his eyes (of joy and emotion, not because we had ruined a good Welsh song) when he came to give his thanks. It was the first time I had been involved in such organised singing and I realised how good a sound can be made when you get 30 or so voices singing collectively, even if individually they are not brilliant.

At Mendip, venues for Ladies Night changed from time to time but I feel the most consistently successful evenings during my time were those held at the Cadbury Country Club. When I first started attending Ladies Nights the Country Club had two main function rooms, one that held about 100 people that was situated near the swimming pool and the other room was the large, main room where the major functions such as cabaret nights (as previously described) would be held. Because of the size of our parties we had the smaller room which was ideal for us and looked splendid when it was fully laid out. I have many great memories of those evenings. I vividly remember John Ledbury's Ladies Night when we put on a spoof "This is Your Life", similar to the popular TV programme, loosely based on John's life inasmuch as he had been a banker, but that is about where fiction took over from fact. My own character from John's "past" was Nathanial West, known as "Nat" to his friends, and for this part I tried to be like a cockney, "wide boy" Arthur Daley by wearing one of my own, very flash cobalt blue check suits and a trilby. Other Table members were also supposedly dodgy people from John's past, presided over by someone speaking in an Irish lilt to impersonate the original and at the time best known presenter Eamonn Andrews, complete with a large red book. Andy Lewis recalls that in his year as Chairman he had been on jury service a short while before Ladies Night and Table remembered this in the cabaret. Roger Burdock, a solicitor in real life, organised a court room drama, with Andy in the dock.

On another occasion, members of Table recreated a cabaret that had been done by our predecessors many years before – a belly dance but with a difference. This involved the members of the cabaret being stood behind a screen that was waste height. Their top halves were bare but had faces painted on them, with the belly button being their pursed lips and large hats covered the whole of their head. Also I believe that the arms were placed "akimbo" to resemble the ears. In time to some music – "I was Kaiser Bill's Batman" by Whistling Jack Smith - they gyrated their "faces" to the music to great effect, particularly as there was a wide variety of stomach sizes from the generous to the skinny. It is my regret that I wasn't asked to participate in this particular cabaret, as it went down as one of the most memorable.

It was customary to mix people up on the dining tables, which was your "party" for the whole evening and I remember at another Ladies Night I was seated for the meal with a new Tabler, Peter Kearnes and his wife Sue, along with other experienced Tablers including Roger Burdock and his wife Jane. Sue was a very attractive, lovely, innocent lady and Peter was a real "wind-up" merchant. During the meal, by way of explaining to Sue who the other various people on the table were, Peter had told Sue that Roger Burdock was a hair-dresser. Roger was in fact a slim, quiet, gentle, balding quintessential solicitor, who was extremely polite and completely unlike any archetypal hair-dresser you could imagine, but Sue bought the line completely.

As was the norm at such functions, during the dancing the men on the table would ask all the other ladies for a dance at some time during the evening and the time duly arrived for Roger to partner Sue. Sue was really non-plussed when she came back to Peter after their dance. "I don't think much of Roger as a hair-dresser" she said, "First of all I asked him what he thought of my hair, and all he said was "very nice". Then I asked him if he thought I should have it long or short and all he could come up with was that he thought it would look nice whichever way I wore it. I don't think I will be going to him to have my hair done, even if he is a friend of yours". It was some time before Peter told Sue what Roger's true occupation was and I'm not sure if Roger ever heard this story, so if he reads this book this might be the first time he has heard this.

As explained earlier, in addition to the small room where we had our Ladies Night, the Cadbury Country Club had a larger room where professional cabaret artists would perform. One year when I was Social Chairman, the then well known local performer Fred Wedlock (he had a chart hit with "The Oldest Swinger In Town") was performing in the main room. Fred was a great supporter of Round Table and appeared at many functions around the Area and I managed to get him to do a half hour stint exclusively for our Ladies Night during the break between his performances in the main room, at a considerably reduced cost. One of our members was a great guy called Ken Shelvey, who at the time was working extremely hard to make a success of his business, and in retrospect it wasn't good planning to have him sat directly in front of Fred. After about ten minutes into Fred's act, which started at about 10.30pm, the wine, the food and a long working week caught up with Ken and he dozed off, well fell asleep, right slap bang in front of Fred. Ever the gentleman, Fred made light of it, used Ken's slumbers in the act and he was a great success. The following weekend we were at another function, not organised by Round Table, but there were many Mendip Tablers there including Ken Shelvey, and again Fred was the cabaret but this time he was the main attraction so had a fairly long stint. Again Ken was sat right at the front and again to everyone's amusement, including Fred's, he fell asleep, although in fairness Ken did manage to last about 20 minutes this time!

Whilst Ladies Nights were arguably the most important social events of the year there were many other events that had to be organised and being a Tabler in two rural areas many of our functions involved being in a barn. In Sittingbourne, shortly after being inducted as a member I and another new member, Cliff Jones, were co-opted onto the Social committee and our first function as a member was a barn dance – that is a dance in a barn as opposed to English Country dancing. Having dossed out the barn with the other members Cliff and my job, as the newest members, was to empty out the portable latrines on the night of the dance! Fortunately Cliff was the manager of the local Boots Chemist and he supplied face masks; it wasn't the best of jobs but everyone had a good laugh about our "job" and it meant we were then accepted completely by the other members.

Shortly after joining Mendip Table one of the first social events on offer was a Strawberry and Champagne Barn Dance. In those days there was a plethora of "pick your own" strawberry farms, which was the cheapest way of buying strawberries and I volunteered to carry out the task of picking the strawberries for the dance. This became my job for a number of years and over time I took my children with me to help with the picking along with Philip Knowles and his boys. This time there were no portable latrines to cope with and the most onerous job we had was a stint behind the bar.

One of the most enjoyable evenings in the calendar at both Sittingbourne and Mendip was the safari supper, although there were slight differences in the organisation of the event between the two clubs. The idea with a safari supper is that everyone taking part would meet at one venue for a welcoming drink. It had been pre-arranged that one set of Tablers (or Ladies

Circler if organised by Ladies Circle) had volunteered to do a starter, another set volunteered to do a main course, a third set will do a pudding and you then end up at a final destination (often the Chairman's house) for coffee and a party, i.e. you go to different venues for all courses.

At Sittingbourne, you drew names out of a hat on the night at the drinks venue as to where you would go for the starter and then again after each course as to where you were to go for the next course, so you had no idea where you were going or who the other guests were going to be at each course until you arrived at the venue. This was great in one way, as that added to the excitement of the whole evening, but the main drawback was that since the venue was a complete lottery, you could end up driving miles if one of the courses was being prepared by someone who lived on one side of the catchment area and another course was being prepared by someone who lived on the other side of the catchment area. In Mendip your venue for the three courses was decided at the drinks party, so you knew exactly where you were going and how long it was going to take you before you set off, and for those so inclined you could also find out who was going to be where. Logistically, this was a far better version, but it did take away some of the fun of the lottery.

At both Sittingbourne and Mendip we had nights where the men prepared the food for the safari supper, which in itself added a different aspect to the evening. In Sittingbourne I volunteered to do a main course, which I recall was chicken and mushroom vol-au-vents with vegetables including new potatoes. I love new potatoes and would generally eat about at least 10 small ones with my meal so on this basis I did enough potatoes for each person to have 10 on their plate. We were catering for eight people so I cooked 80 new potatoes! At the time my mother was our regular baby sitter (my father had died six months before my first child, Mathew was born) and she helped me prepare the potatoes. In the terrines on the table they seemed to be everywhere and needless to say no-one apart from me ate 10 potatoes, with the average being about 5. It became a huge joke and guests were taking them on to the next venue in bags in an effort to help me out. It was certainly a talking point at the final party.

Unfortunately sometimes the pudding course was so enjoyable and you were so comfortable that some people never made it to the final party. This happened to Linda and me in Sittingbourne when we went for pudding at a notoriously good host's house. In those days, shamefully people weren't so concerned about drinking and driving, particularly in such a rural environment and by the time we had arrived for pudding we all had had a number of glasses of wine. More wine was handed out with the pudding, for some reason a joke telling competition started and the whole occasion was just supremely funny with the only completely sober person there, a heavily pregnant lady, worried she was going to give birth on the spot as she laughed so much. We all decided that going to the final party was out of the question and had coffee, mints and a glass of port, more jokes and went home.

As already intimated, Mendip Table was a very family orientated club. Children were always included in virtually everything we did but the most enjoyable events that were put on by Round Table specifically with children in mind were Father's Day bar-b-ques and monthly Sunday pub visits. That's not to say that other events weren't organised, such as visits to the local pantomime at Christmas time and children's Christmas parties but they tended to be organised by Ladies Circle for the children of Tablers rather than by Tablers ourselves.

The Father's Day bar-b-ques tended to be on the sand dunes at Berrow Beach, near Weston-super-Mare or on the beach at Weston itself and were always well attended and popular. Philip Avery produced an oil drum cut in half that acted as a giant grill and everyone brought food to cook or sandwiches – it didn't matter what you did, everything was accepted. Kate Fielder, wife of Roger, was a professional caterer and I recall their family turning up with foie gras left over from a previous night's function, compared to our ham sandwiches. Then there was Roger and Jane Burdock, with Jane turning up complete with china teapot and tea set. I liked it when the venue was on Berrow Beach; my daughter Stephanie would get tired (and irritable!) but refused to go to sleep but as the beach was long and flat I could put her in the car and drive up and down for five minutes, which was guaranteed to send her off. There would invariably be entertainment in the form of cricket, rounders or football and one memorable year there was a kite-flying competition with people encouraged to come up with the most unusual kite. As usual David Brown came up with the maddest idea – a 2x2 concrete floor slab with ropes attached to it that he inveigled various Tablers to pick up and run with along the sands, throwing it up in the air in an obviously vain attempt to get it airborne. Another kite that seemed doom to failure was produced by Jon Andrewes, which was made from an old shirt, but he surprised everyone by getting it to stay up in the air.

On another occasion we relocated Father's Day to Steep Holme, a privately owned island in the Bristol Channel, about 5 miles offshore from Weston. Once you are there you will get fantastic, 360degree panoramic views of the Bristol Channel and the Somerset and Welsh coastlines and is well worth a visit. The problem is, of course that to get there you have to go over water in a small boat, which for people like my wife Linda, and to a lesser extent David Brown, is purgatory as both of them have a fear of water. Indeed, although the sea was like a millpond on the return journey Linda got sea-sick, which brought on a migraine, which made her rather unwell for several hours.

I believe it was when David Brown was Social Chairman that he came up with the idea of a "Pub-a-Month". Each month David would pick a pub in the region that was children friendly and we would all turn up, some just to have a drink and others to lunch as well. It needs to be remembered that this was about 28 years ago long before it was fashionable for whole families to meet up and go to pubs, so it really was quite innovative. Again, this was a very popular event, very well supported and looked forward to by Tablers, wives and children alike. Indeed, I recall going to a parents' evening at my son Mathew's school and being greeted by the teacher with "Hello, according to Mathew you lead a wonderful life, going to the pub every week". It transpired that all the children at school in Mathew's class had to keep a journal and Mathew often wrote with great affection of going to the pub. It was obvious the teacher was amused by the whole thing, realised that was not our actual lifestyle and thought the idea of whole families going along on a social occasion such as that was a great idea.

Membership of and enjoyment in Round Table should not be dictated by the wealth of the individual and everyone I have known in Round Table has been conscious to keep all functions within an affordable price so that everyone can attend at least one of the functions put on. Obviously some people will be financially better off than others but the idea was to put on a number of affordable functions such that people can pick and chose which to attend, not be forced to attend only the cheap ones. Clearly Ladies Night was usually the most expensive social event of the year and also excluded children, but there were other functions in addition to those already mentioned that were put on and could be attended with little cost, such as the fireworks party on Bonfire Night. Although this was essentially put on for the children, very often childless Tablers would attend and have just as good a time. During my time Roger Fielder was invariably the host for this function and in addition to a roaring bonfire and fireworks, there would be roast potatoes and other such traditional food and drink available. Even if it rained, which it seemed to do most years, the event would still take place and would be in addition to any official school or village function that were almost obligatory, so the success was in the company irrespective of the weather.

Another such event was the "Piston Broke" trophy, a car treasure hunt that always seemed to be won by Ken and Sue Brown. This was the classic treasure hunt, with people given clues as to where to go to certain landmarks and then recall what they saw, with points being awarded for the number of landmarks noted. It wasn't really a timed event, as we didn't want people driving recklessly merely to win the trophy, a polished broken car piston mounted on a wooden plinth, but there were extra points awarded for the quickest time taken to collect all the clues and there would be a number of "trials" en route such as reversing into a tight space or judging the narrowest distance you could drive your car between two poles. This was another event where children could accompany their parent if they so wished and often would end at the Chairman's house for social drinks.

Those were the main, regular social events that filled our calendar and in addition we had one off events that were done on the whim of the social Chairman for that particular year. One particular function that most chairmen had was a Christmas party at their house. This would range from an "at home" where it would be open house for the day where Tablers popped in, with or without children for a festive drink, to a full blown evening party for grown-ups only with a buffet and dancing. There would also be summer bar-b-ques and skittles evenings. I have very fond memories of a 1960's evening that I was involved in where, with the help of Graham Dawes who at the time had a post office in Wookie, we spent many happy hours recording about six hours of 60s music onto cassettes. On the evening of the event we took it in turns to be the disc jockey, complete with cheesey introductions to the songs.

Although this is essentially a story about Round Tablers and their exploits, it should also be remembered that Ladies Circle had their own social events that, generally all Round Tablers and their partners were invited to, irrespective as to whether or not their wife was in ladies Circle, and these added to the number of social occasions available to attend in a year. One of the most enjoyable of these functions that spring to mind was a dinner party that Liz Bull held in her house early in her year as Ladies Circle chairlady, although on this particular occasion it was Circlulars and their husbands only, as it was meant to be Liz welcoming her members to her year. It seemed everyone invited attended and there were about 50 of us formally sat down. To get a particularly large table in the house Liz had a window removed, as it was too big to go in through the normal route. We were sat effectively all together although in three different areas with tables joining the dining room, into the hall and into the lounge. At the beginning of the evening each lady and gentleman was invited to pick a name out of one of two hats, one hat for a man and one for a lady, with each name representing one of a couple, for example the man might pick out the name Troilus and the lady picked out a piece of paper with the name Cressida on it, or Romeo and Juliet. Before dinner commenced each individual had to find their "partner" and it was that person you sat next to for dinner. This idea really broke the ice with everyone joining in and the evening was a huge success.

The last of the social events that should be mentioned, particularly at the *end* of this section, is "hand-over" evening. As previously explained, a Table year runs from April to April and in March the last formal meeting takes place where new officers are elected and a new Chairman takes over. 31 March is also when those Tablers who are no longer eligible to be members under the age rule formally leave the organisation, and the last meeting in the Table year is when the Chairmanship is formally handed over and presentations made to the retiring Tablers. The normal gift for the retirees is an engraved beer tanker but sometimes if the member has done something exceptional during his table career then an additional gift is given. As I was also an officer at Area level, I was given a tankard by Area in recognition of my service.

In both Tables where I have been a member, there would be a meal at the beginning of the meeting and no other Round Table business was carried out at hand-over night. It was also customary for the retiring Tablers to provide some entertainment after the presentations have been made and very often this entertainment would be in the form of a stripper. I have already explained that at Mendip we looked after our own bar, and it was at this stage that I usually volunteered to be the steward for the rest of the evening and go behind the bar where you were safe from being picked on by the stripper to help with her act. Other guys were not so bashful, however and were very happy to participate and the stories that have come out of these meetings are legendary - but what went on behind closed doors stays behind closed doors!

As already stated earlier, I left Round Table under the age rule in 1987 at the same time as Peter Smith, Bob Hughes and Dick Thatcher. Philip Avery was due to leave at the same time but as he was Chairman in his final year he automatically received an extra honorary year. To mark our years in Table the four who left in 1987 went with our wives to Paris, Bob and me with our wives Felicity and Linda in one car and Peter and Dick with their wives Pauline and Angela in another car.

It was my first trip to Paris and it was a really good break, taking in all the usual tourist sites and eating and drinking well. At the time it was possible to get a hovercraft across the channel and the trip over was very

From left (bystander), Dick Thatcher, Pauline Smith, Angela, Linda and me in Paris. Peter Smith is taking the picture. Bob and Felicity had gone off on their own.

calm. However, the return trip was very rough; indeed we were the last crossing before the route was closed due to safety reasons. It wasn't so bad while the hovercraft hugged the coastline, but as soon as it went into open water the crossing became like a bad aeroplane crossing, with deep troughs as the craft went up and down waves. Poor Felicity was particularly bad and Linda wasn't much better but even with the bad journey back it was a fitting end to my Table life.

NATIONAL AND INTERNATIONAL EVENTS

As already intimated, Round Table is enjoyed both nationally and internationally and events are put on to reflect this. At a national level, there was a National Sporting Weekend organised annually and despite Chris Wardman's insistence that it wasn't just for those who were gifted in the sporting sense I never went to this event on the basis that I just wasn't good enough at sport to compete. Chris went many times to this weekend, often accompanied by Steve Wilkinson. The first time Chris went he represented our Area at swimming but such was the stiffness of the competition that thereafter he competed in what he called "community" sports that were created merely to get people involved.

It was at the Sheffield Area Sports Weekend that

"Eric" was born, a fictitious person who was allegedly parading around the room when food was served and therefore not at his place at the table for his meal. Thus "Eric" was served his food, which was then distributed amongst the rest of the people on the table. Every time thereafter when there was an empty place at a function we would say "that's Eric's place" to get food laid up to be shared out by the rest of us.

Generally the entertainment at these events was excellent with the exception of two instances. All the delegates were at the Crucible in Sheffield where a nationally known comedian was giving a performance. However he decided to pick on one section of the audience for the butt of some of his jokes, which upset the whole audience to the extent that he was booed off stage – an example of the strength of the fellowship amongst Tablers. The other occasion was at Birmingham and involved a mind reader, but his act was so weak that people saw through it.

The largest event in the Round Table calendar is the National Conference, held annually at venues throughout the UK. Naturally with numbers of members of Round Table in decline the event is not as big as it was, but it is still a huge occasion, involving several thousands of people. The event would be staged over four days with a welcome party on Thursday evening, an International lunch on Friday with a

President's banquet and ball in the evening. On Saturday would be the actual Conference that would start at about 11.30am and end about 5.00pm. At this conference members of the National Council or individual delegates would present motions that could involve changes to rules, standing orders, or even the actual make up of membership (e.g. changing the upper age limit from age 40 to 45). The National Conference has already been mentioned earlier in this book when Mendip Chairman Richard Harill made an impassioned appeal for the Axbridge Air disaster. Each speaker is given a limited amount of time to speak and Richard had to be given special exemption to deliver his speech in full. The standard of debate is exceptionally high, often with great humour and it takes a lot of confidence to make a speech in that setting. On Saturday evening there is traditionally a fancy dress ball where often each Area attending has their own theme and on Sunday the delegates depart for home after breakfast. Many Tablers attend just the conference without going to all the social events and if any Tabler reading this book has never been I would urge everyone to go at least once. The level of detail given to the organising of the four days is outstanding and if the conference itself is of no interest it is worth going just to admire the logistics that have gone into the organisation.

Personally, I went to three National Conferences,

Manchester, Yarmouth and Bournemouth, and attended the conference only at Birmingham. Manchester in 1982 was notable for many reasons, both good and bad. Three couples went from Mendip Round Table in two cars; Peter and Pauline Smith went on their own and Jeff and June Douce and Linda and I went in Jeff's car. We stayed in a hotel close to Manchester station that didn't have a car park and on one of the mornings (I forget which) we woke up to find Pete's car had been stolen. It was eventually recovered a few weeks later, burnt out, and thus we all had to travel home in Jeff's car packed like sardines. That obviously put a dampener on the weekend, but I recall that it was a really good event. As was usual with these occasions, the organising committee had commandeered a large number of the local buses, which went around the various "official" hotels picking up Tablers and taking them to the event venues, free of charge and then would be available after the event to take us home again. On the night of the President's Ball we all got dressed in our finery and found we were the only ones on the bus going to the venue, a huge marquee not far from the spot where Pope John Paul II had recently addressed thousands of people in Heaton Park. Unfortunately we had a bus driver who had no idea how to get into the park and he drove around, stopping various unsuspecting members of the public for directions, but to no avail. Eventually we asked to be dropped off outside the park at a spot where we could see the marquee and walked across the wet grass, having climbed over a fence in our best gear, arriving in a not very good mood. We managed to get back to the hotel OK and next night went with many others to the fancy dress party. I shall never forget the look on some drunk's face who jumped on the bus on the way home thinking it was a normal bus in service, to be confronted with the rest of the "passengers" all in different fancy dress costumes. He quickly got off.

The National conference in Yarmouth was best remembered for the appalling weather and equally appalling guest house that we stayed in. Whilst Yarmouth was used to entertaining holidaymakers, at the time it did not have a great number of hotels and thus many conference delegates were staying in guest houses and I would imagine we were just unlucky with ours. It seemed that all the jokes relating to guest house landladies applied to our hosts. They were reluctant to let us have house keys so that we could come back late in the evening and insisted that breakfast would be at 08.30 in the morning, which would be on the table regardless as to whether we would be up. Needless to say, at least one couple did not make it for 08.30 – Pete and Pauline Smith – and there was an uncomfortable atmosphere while we reasoned with our hosts to give them a few minutes leeway. Pete eventually emerged but he was none too pleased with the way he had been treated.

Bournemouth was a good venue and, although I can't remember all who went I do recall that there was a good turnout from Mendip. Whatever the fancy dress theme was I recall David Brown having a very high hat on. For some reason he became detached from his wife Dee when it came time to go home and I recall being on a bus going back to the hotel and seeing Dave charging along the pavement with his tall hat swaying from side to side, oblivious to the local passers by going in the opposite direction. I am informed that Dave and Dee (along with Chris and Wendy Wardman) also went to the conference in Glasgow, where the famous 1960's band The Merseybeats had been the entertainment for the Friday night ball. They happened to be staying in the same hotel as the Browns and on the morning of the National Conference Dee was outside the hotel waiting for a bus when the group came out. Seeing Dee waiting they gave her a lift to the National Conference venue, a very nice gesture. That night all four went to the Fancy Dress ball, with Dave and Chris dressed in Somerset Smocks with tartan wellies. At the Isle of Man conference the Browns and Wardmans again attended where the fancy dress theme was "Fantasy Island". Our crew went as Alice in Wonderland characters, with most as cards. Andy Lewis recalls also attending the National Conference at the Isle of Man where there was a really good turn out from Mendip, which was really enjoyable but which will unfortunately be likely to be remembered for the wrong reason – the appalling standard of the first hotel allocated to them. Fortunately they managed to find an alternative hotel, which was fine and they enjoyed the rest of the conference.

The National Conference at Birmingham was where the Chairman of our Area (Area 12), Hugo King was to become National President. I can't recall if any of Mendip attended the conference apart from the actual Saturday Conference but I do recall a number of us, including me, went only to the conference to see Hugo sworn in. David Brown was one of those who went with me and, as David had spent some time working in Birmingham we took his guide after the Conference as to where we should have a drink before going home, I believe in the Aston area. One of the TV adverts featured at the time was for a drink called "Babycham" a sparkling Perry marketed with pioneering television advertisements to appeal specifically to women. It was the first alcoholic product to be advertised on UK television, the campaign being launched in 1957, and was originally marketed as a "genuine champagne Perry". The advert at the time featured a couple walking into a cheerfully noisy, crowded bar and as they walk in the noise descends to a hush. The lady in the advert says to her partner "I'll have a Babycham" and immediately the bar returns to the happy state it was in before. When we got to the pub in Aston, we walked in to be greeted by the sight of a mass of what looked like hairy bikers and, as in the TV advert, the room became quiet. David obviously picked up on the occasion and said, what seemed quietly to me but to this day I don't know if anyone else heard it, "I'll have a Babycham". I started laughing and, miraculously, the room became loud again, but discretion proved the better part of valor and we turned round, walked out and found another place to have our quiet drink.

The National Association of Round Tables was a member of WOCO – the World Council of Service Clubs and each year there was an annual conference at a different venue throughout the world. Any member of Round Table was eligible to attend but as the cost could be prohibitive for many Tablers invariably The National Association would fund the cost of one Tabler and his wife to attend the conference, wherever it was in the world. This would be done by the organization of a raffle, with the draw usually made at the UK Annual National Conference. Chris and Wendy Wardman were fortunate to attend two WOCO conferences by this method. The first conference they attended was in Dublin, but in this case Chris was the only Tabler wanting to go and so won the "raffle" by default. The second trip, however, was an altogether different story, as the conference was to take place in Zimbabwe, with many Tablers wanting to win the prize. The draw was at the International lunch at the Brighton conference and at the time of the draw Wendy was in the ladies' loo and so missed the result, not believing Chris when she returned to the lunch table. It really was a splendid prize to win, as it included the WOCO conference itself, including flights, a pre-conference tour of Zimbabwe, Harare, Bulawayo, Hwange National Park, Victoria Falls also including overnight trips as well. The trip was made even more enjoyable, as a couple of lads from Blackwood made the trip under their own steam.

As far as most Mendip Tablers were concerned, however, the most important part of International Tabling was our twinning with Cholet Table in France, in the Loire Valley. Cholet stands on an eminence on the right bank of the Moine, which used to be crossed by a bridge from the fifteenth century. It is about 50 km southeast of Nantes with a population of about 55,000, famous for the manufacture of linen and handkerchiefs. We would try and have one visit between Mendip Round Table and Cholet Round Table each Table year, alternating between Mendip and Cholet, but this did not always prove possible. The twin was established about 15 years after Mendip was formed, when Nick Barrington and Colin Davies decided to conduct a survey of suitable Tables in France with which to twin. Once it was established the twinning proved to be very popular, with many Tablers and their wives making their way across The English Channel to France or across La Manche to England every time a visit was arranged.

Whilst it seemed the standard of wealth amongst French Tablers was higher than their British counterparts, they also seemed a lot more relaxed – about everything – than us. They were certainly very generous hosts whenever a visit was made and were always good company. Their relaxed attitude sometimes made it difficult for us when it was our turn to host, as often right up to the last minute we would not know how many

French Tablers were to be hosted and when they were arriving. I sometimes believed that there was unfortunately an element of competition – only on our part I feel – as to what we could put on to entertain them compared to what hospitality we had received last time we visited them. Nonetheless, despite all this (which in all probability was all in my own mind and didn't exist at all) every visit made either to Cholet or as us as the hosts always went off exceptionally well. Indeed, many friendships were formed that are still strong today.

Earlier in this book I have described what for me was one of the highlights of my Table years, the six-man bike ride to Cholet, but there were many other stories associated with the visits, such as Terry Humberstone teaching the French how to sing "the Music Man", complete with mouth instruments. Chris Wardman was a particularly strong supporter of the Cholet twinning and he recalls on one trip he and Andy Lewis were to stay with one of the Cholet stalwarts, Alain Carraiou. As they did not know the area, Chris stopped and asked a policeman the way, only to be given an escort all the way to Alain's house. The following year when Chris organised the return trip, there was a formal reception in Hutton Court, the summer residence of the Bishop of Bath and Wells, with local band British Bulldog as entertainment. Andy Lewis recalls that in his year as Chairman it was Mendip's turn to visit Cholet and they presented Cholet Table with a sketch of caricatures of our Mendip Tablers at the time, done by a local artist in

Axbridge. Andy recalls this as being a brilliant idea by Jon Andrewes that went down particularly well and Andy's speech in French contained one embarrassing faux par, but he was reluctant to explain what it was!

Tableau of all Mendip Tablers in 1991 painted by local artist being presented by Mendip Chairman Andy Lewis to Cholet President Jean-Jaques Moreau June 1991.

Apart from the bike ride I did not carry out any other visits to Cholet but I participated fully when they visited us and I have two great memories of such visits. The first is when Linda and I hosted a dinner party at our house. I can't recall exactly how many combined Mendip and Cholet Tablers and their wives we were hosting but as we do not have the largest of dining rooms we moved the dining table into the lounge and put another table alongside it to seat them all. Unfortunately, apart from Luc and Helene Gilbert from Cholet and Bob and Felicity Hughes from Mendip I am unable to recall the other guests. As already explained, Cholet was famous for its linen and Bob and Felicity Hughes supplied a large table cloth that had been purchased from Cholet on a previous visit. I think the lack of space actually added to the occasion, as the French seemed genuinely grateful for the trouble we had gone to and the evening went off so well that it was gone midnight before we went to the final party.

Linda had prepared a fantastic chocolate desert that our guests from Cholet adored and after desert we had cheese and biscuits (much to the surprise of the French who have their cheese before desert) followed by coffee and liqueurs. Bob had a brandy and he was just about to light a cigar when one of our French lady guests stopped him and took it away from him. She then asked if we had a candle, which of course we were able to provide, and the candle was lit. She then hoisted up her skirt and rolled the cigar up and down her thigh, gazing all the time into Bob's eyes. She then dipped the cigar in Bob's brandy and dried off the surplus brandy by placing the cigar in her mouth and seductively pushing and pulling the cigar in and out of her mouth. After that she held the cigar over the candle flame until it was alight whereupon she handed the cigar to Bob and said in a low, husky voice "There Bob, it is now ready for you", by which time Bob was positively drooling and the rest of the table laughing. It didn't prove easy for poor Bob to smoke his cigar, but he did say afterwards that it was one of the most enjoyable he had had and that he hoped the English ladies present, and particularly Felicity, had taken note.

The other momentous evening was at a combined black tie dinner and dance for the Cholet guests at the Sidcot Hotel where there were about 70 joint French and English present. The English Chairman was Philip Avery who was not comfortable giving a speech in French and so his secretary, Dick Thatcher, suggested that Philip gave his speech in English and he would translate as he went along. It is difficult to put on paper the hilarious consequences of these actions but the whole audience was in uproar throughout the speech and both Philip and Dick received a standing ovation at the end. Dick did a fair job translating the words spoken by Philip but where he didn't know the exact French word he used a mixture of English in a French accent and Franglais, all with a dead-pan face, which is what caused all the mirth. The Sidcot is a working hotel and they were particularly busy on the night of our ball, particularly for some reason with honeymoon couples – three in all on that night. When the first couple arrived they were serenaded by the French contingent and escorted to their room, and they took their unexpected "entertainment" fairly well. The next couple were treated to the same behaviour and they also took it quite well, albeit with a little less good humour than the first couple. Unfortunately by the time the third honeymoon couple arrived the hour was quite late and a lot more wine had been consumed and, not content with just serenading the couple, they decided to carry the bride up to their suite and go in with them. As can be imagined, this was not so well received and it did quite upset the bride so an apology had to be made and I believe a compensatory bottle of something sent to their room. Ignoring the last incident however, the whole evening was a huge success and will go down in the annals of Mendip Round Table as one of the great hosting events.

"HIGH OFFICE"

In Round Table, be it at local level, Area level or nationally, the highest offices were Treasurer, Secretary, Vice Chairman and Chairman. All the other jobs such as the fund raising Chairman and social Chairman were extremely important posts but the offices mentioned above were the backbone of the club and most aspiring chairmen would reckon to do these jobs on their way to becoming Chairman, as they give an insight into how the club works.

Unless the day job of an individual was in finance such as banking or accountancy, probably the most difficult job for many Tablers was as Treasurer. This person controls the finances of the individual club and will often have a minimum of 2 but usually more bank accounts to manage. There would generally be one account for the day to day running of the club, with a separate Charity account for the charitable funds that are raised. Other accounts might be established for special events, such as a Cholet account (for the trip to or visit from Cholet Round Table) and historically The Axbridge Disaster account or the Italian Earthquake account, although over the years there have been many more individual, special accounts set up and subsequently closed. He would be responsible for all monetary transactions in and out of the club including any payments that might be necessary at an ordinary meeting. He would also be responsible for calculating and proposing and subsequently collecting the annual member fees to cover the costs of capitation fees, meals and other possible expenses necessary to run the club.

This job can be made even more difficult depending on how the club is set up. For example, when I was Treasurer in Sittingbourne Round Table the meal fees were collected on the night, whereas in Mendip they were collected by a monthly standing order so the only meal fees that the Treasurer had to collect in Mendip on the night of a meeting were guest meals. Also when I was Treasurer, in 1975, it was more of a cash society than prevails now and since it was the Treasurer's sole responsibility for the management of funds I was often inundated with cash from all angles at the end of a meeting. This was particularly true if there had been a fund raising event or a forthcoming social event and members wanted to hand in the proceeds of their event or pay for the tickets for the social occasion. There were cash and cheques coming at me from all angles and it was a wonder that I came even close to balancing the books at the end of the year. As it was I was fortunate to have a very nice accountant in Table by the name of Gerald Bishop who helped me get the accounts together for presentation at the end of the Table year but even then I made such a pig's ear of it that I was elected Treasurer the following year so that I could get it right next time! I was heartened to learn when I came to Mendip Table that I was in illustrious company in that none other than George Berry had just about as much trouble as I did with that role.

The role of Secretary is just as important but I found it far less stressful. The secretary is basically the Chairman's right hand man and it is helpful if they get on well together. As already mentioned when I was Chairman I was fortunate to have David Brown as my secretary, which made my year far less stressful. As secretary you are privileged to know all that is going on not only in your own Table but throughout your Area and even nationally because in theory all correspondence goes to the secretary, which he would then delegate to the appropriate sub-chairman such as the fund raising chairman, social chairman etc to deal with whatever subjects the incoming post had thrown up. The secretary is responsible for getting the agenda together for the normal bi-monthly meeting and handling all the correspondence. Before the meeting, if there was to be a speaker he would work with the speaker secretary to ensure that the speaker had any equipment that he needed to fulfil his presentation. This was crucial when I was in Table when the usual visual aides were slides and a projector was needed (often the speaker would not have one of their own) whereas in the present day any presentation would usually be by lap-top thus all that is needed is a blank wall or some such surface. Indeed, many establishments where Round Table meetings are held now have state of the art equipment all installed for such occurrences. At the end of the Table year it is the responsibility of the secretary to ensure that the AGM goes smoothly, that there are candidates for all the positions that will be vacated and therefore need to be filled for the next Table year, voting slips are available where appropriate and the voting is fair and above board. It is also his responsibility to ensure that tankards have been ordered and suitably engraved for presentation to the retiring Tablers and that the Chairman's jewel has been correctly ordered. Along with the other officers he will be expected to make a speech summing up his year and his year is not finally done until the meeting is closed. It is possible to miss out being secretary or treasurer before becoming Chairman but it certainly helps if you have carried out these positions because they give you great insight and understanding of the machinations of Round Table in general and your own club in particular, and I believe makes the job of Chairman easier and therefore more enjoyable.

The highlight of many a Tabler's life in Round Table was to become Chairman of their own Club, or even higher, such as Area Chairman or the highest honour of all, National President. I am sure there will be someone who will know better, but I never knew of any Area Chairman or National President who had not at one time been Chairman at Club level. Not every member gets the opportunity to have the honour of becoming Chairman and whilst it is generally the highlight for those that do, for some who get to Chairman it is not always a happy year. I feel very sad for those men who do not enjoy their year as Chairman, particularly as I had a wonderful time and can imagine how much they had been looking forward to taking over the Chair. It was not a position they took on lightly and it can end up tainting their feelings of what was probably a very happy period in their lives as members of Round Table.

As already intimated, the usual route for most members was to do all, or the majority of jobs in Round Table such as secretary, Treasurer, fund raising officer, sports and social etc before becoming Chairman. Most guys in Table left being Chairman until near the end of their Table life, this being the pinnacle of their time in Table and many felt, me included, that after having held that office there was little to match the enjoyment they had as Chairman. Obviously if an individual wanted to go onto being Area Chairman or National President then he would aim to be Chairman of his own Table earlier, particularly as he would normally be expected to hold various offices on Area or National executive before becoming Vice Chairman and then Chairman of Area or Vice President and then President Nationally. However, since the average age for joining Round Table in my day was age 35, for many people they didn't have the time to reach Chairman of their own Table, let alone go onto higher office in Area or National. When I was in Sittingbourne Table, there was one man who became Chairman twice, Lynn Davies, but he joined at the age of 18. However, as far as I am aware he never had aspirations to go onto Area or National, he just got enormous enjoyment from Tabling locally.

Before becoming Chairman an individual is voted at the AGM to Vice Chairman with the understanding that, generally, after one year as Vice Chairman he will become Chairman, unopposed. I stood for Vice Chairman three years before I was due to retire from Table, which meant I would have one year as Vice Chairman, one year as Chairman and then one year as Immediate Past Chairman before formally leaving the organization, which was ideal for me. However, when I was thinking as standing for Vice Chairman there was another individual who was thinking about being Chairman, Terry Humberstone, and as he was a year older than me, this was his last chance to stand for the Chair. As in theory I still had one more year to try for the Chair I decided that if Terry wanted to stand I would not oppose him and would then try again the following year, which would also be my last chance. In the event, circumstances decided Terry against trying for the position as Vice Chairman so I stood for the position and was very fortunate to be elected.

Vice Chairman is probably the easiest job in Table, unless you are unfortunate enough to have something happen to your Chairman in the middle of his year that forces him to resign as Chairman or take leave of absence, when the Vice Chairman will normally take over his duties for the rest of the year. In these circumstances the acting Chairman is usually given the option of continuing as Chairman for what would have been his "normal" year, so that he can do the things that he probably had planned to do rather than fulfill someone else's ideas. It is very rare that a Chairman doesn't fulfill his year and therefore the job of Vice Chairman is usually a fairly leisurely one where many Vice Chairmen take the opportunity to be members of the other committees (fund raising, community service etc), attend Area meetings and accompany the Chairman on any visits he might undertake. He will also run the meetings if the Chairman is unable to attend and if there is a special project that needs to be undertaken it is likely he will be the lead. I don't know if it is a national tradition, but in Mendip it was the Vice Chairman who proposed the toast to the Ladies at Ladies Night. For many Vice Chairmen this was the scariest part of their year.

And so having been secretary, treasurer, Chairman of Fundraising, Community Service and Social, and having completed your year as Vice Chairman, the time has finally come to that time in the AGM when the current Chairman hopefully sits down to thunderous applause having delivered his farewell speech and hands over the Chain of Office to you, and you are finally Chairman. For most people this is a fairly emotional time and very often the first speech is not the best he will ever make. For some reason known only to myself (well actually it was because I saw someone else do it very successfully), I decided my opening words would be sung and I had even gone to the trouble of going to Roger Burdock's wife, who was a music teacher, to have a few singing lessons. Needless to say, it was a disaster and after just a handful of bars I gave up trying to sing and resorted to speaking. Fortunately it seems I was quickly forgiven and it was never mentioned again.

The year I was Chairman lived up to all my expectations. The only slight reservation had nothing to do with the Chairmanship and everything to do with my life outside Round Table in that at work I was in the process of establishing myself with a new employer and therefore I had this extra problem to deal with that I would rather have not had. Within Table it was as good as it could be. I had a great team around me, particularly my secretary David Brown, and, as already mentioned, I was fortunate to be Chairman on our 25th anniversary. This involved the great bike ride to Cholet and the Anniversary dinner, both of which have already been described. We continued our fund raising efforts, carried out our community service work and had good social and sports activities and I had great fun attending if not all then the majority of these events. At the end of my year, in my closing speech, I reflected that my predecessor, Peter Smith, had said that people in the room could probably have done the job of Chairman better, but none could have had as much enjoyment as he did during his year. I commented that possibly every Chairman could say the same thing, and Peter's words certainly reflected my own feelings. I also recalled the various visits we had made throughout the year on table nights to Thatchers Cider Farm, Wilton Wine Groves and another trip to Blackwood Table to sample once again their particular brand of hospitality, and visits outside Table nights as families to The Big Pit at Blaenavon and the Cardiff Searchlight Tattoo.

As Chairman of Mendip we had the privilege of handing out awards to individual members at the end of our year. Each Table will have its own trophies to give out but at the end of my year I made the following presentations:

"Piss-up" Trophy – although there was no obvious candidate to give it in the truest sense of the award, I made the presentation to David Brown who attended every social event bar one – the Barn Dance – missed only because his wife was so obviously pregnant.

Dick Thatcher was presented with the wooden spoon for his Minutes and acerbic wit and barbed comments during the meetings.

On the sporting front there was the Martin Bull Trophy to be awarded and this went to Mike Peel, who at the National Sporting weekend when as probably the smallest bloke in Table he was in the tug-of-war team.

The Fellowship Trophy was presented to Ray Cowlin who at the time was relatively new to Round Table but who joined and immediately threw himself wholeheartedly into our activities, attending the majority of the functions that had been arranged.

In addition, as Chairman I attended the Area meetings, which heightened my awareness and enjoyment of the wider movement that persuaded me to get involved as Area Extension Officer in my final year in Table. I am not vain enough to think that my year as Chairman would have been outstandingly memorable if it had not been for it being the 25th Anniversary year, but I had a thoroughly wonderful time, I don't think I upset too many people in the process and I believe I left Philip Avery, who succeeded me as Chairman, with Mendip Table in as good a shape as I inherited it as Chairman.

FINALE

I feel that the years around which I was a member of Round Table - 1970 to 1990 – were the "golden" years of Tabling, although I dare say our predecessors probably thought the same. That said, in 1960 an analysis of the ages in Tables in Area 12 (the area to which Mendip belonged) was taken and a sample of the results are shown:

Table	Membership	Average Age	Remarks
Bath	55	33.5	8 aged 30
Bristol	99	32.1	7 aged 25
Weston	38	34	

This came from a book written about the history of Bristol Round Table No. 9 around 1962, which also states there were 23,000 Tablers in 783 Tables. At its peak, there were around 1300 different clubs in Great Britain with around 26,000 members. As at 2012 there are about 510 clubs with around 5,400 members. Sadly my own Table in Mendip closed in December 2001 after 42 years (coincidentally roughly the age at which a Tabler would have originally retired if he was given an honorary year's membership at the end of his time) with the remaining members, of which there were about four, transferring back to the mother Table, Weston-super-Mare. My first Table, Sittingbourne and Milton is still going but as at 2012 their website shows them as being down to 5 members. Since my time in Table it seems that the demands on young men have increased considerably resulting in fewer and fewer joining such organizations and numbers have declined dramatically, although the RTBI President stated in February 2013 that they hoped to welcome 700 new members in 2013. To my mind they are missing out on great opportunities. Not only does membership generally help an individual develop but, certainly in my own case, I did things that I would never have done in my everyday life, the majority of which I hope have been chronicled here.

I hope this book has done justice to the organisation known as RTBI and that I have managed to achieve part of my objective in writing it - of trying to bring Round Table to life, to try and get across the joy, fun and satisfaction we had in Round Table as individuals and families. As I said in the preface to this book, Round Table is in my opinion the greatest club ever formed for young men and I will be eternally grateful to the organisation for the opportunities it gave me, the number of interesting people I have met as a result of being a member, the great friendships it has helped me form and the way it has shaped my life.

APPENDIX 1

List of Mendip Round Table founder members

Ken Atkins

Ron Barron

Chris Brice

Bill Burge

Bernard Cleave

Peter Duckett

Robert Edwards

David Henderson

Bob Hill

John Horne

Dick House

Jim Lukins

Harold McBride

Dennis Malpass

Brian Mellor

John Milton

Bryan Patterson

Richard Patterson

Bill Phippen

Geoff Rodway

Keith Smith

George Standen

Ivor Standen

APPENDIX 2

List of Mendip Round Table Chairmen

1959-60	K Millman	1980-81	I Leavey
1960-61	G Standen, B Cleave	1981-82	J Ledbury
1961-62	B J Patterson	1982-83	W Oxenham
1962-63	K Atkins	1983-84	J Douce
1963-64	D W Malpass	1984-85	P Smith
1964-65	D N Evans	1985-86	E Parlour
1965-66	R Brown	1986-87	P Avery
1966-67	D S Johnson	1987-88	C Wardman
1967-68	B W J Lovell	1988-89	P Knowles
1968-69	P Edwards	1989-90	D Brown
1969-70	J A H Lukins	1990-91	M Hagen
1970-71	G Berry	1991-92	A Lewis
1971-72	M G Phillips	1992-93	J Andrewes
1972-73	J Horne	1993-94	C Black
1973-74	R Harrill	1994-95	M Newman
1974-75	T Bridgman	1995-96	A Jones
1975-76	S Tilley	1996-97	J Mitchell
1976-77	J Morse	1997-98	T Small
1977-78	K Shelvey	1998-99	A Flint
1978-79	J Rose	1999-00	J Broughton
1979-80	N Williams	2000-01	T Quantick